The Harlem Renaissance

Other titles in the American History series

AMERICAN HISTORY

The Harlem Renaissance

Stuart A. Kallen

LUCENT BOOKS
A part of Gale, Cengage Learning

GALE
CENGAGE Learning

Detroit • New York • San Francisco • New Haven, Conn • Waterville, Maine • London

LIBRARY OF CONGRESS CATALOGING-IN-PUBLICATION DATA

Kallen, Stuart A., 1955-
  The Harlem Renaissance / by Stuart A. Kallen.
    p. cm. — (American history)
  Includes bibliographical references and index.
  ISBN 978-1-4205-0104-9 (hardcover)
  1. African Americans—Intellectual life—20th century—Juvenile literature.
2. Harlem Renaissance—Juvenile literature. 3. African American arts—
20th century—Juvenile literature. 4. African Americans—History—
1877-1964—Juvenile literature. 5. Harlem (New York, N.Y.)—Intellectual
life—20th century—Juvenile literature. 6. African Americans—New York
(State)—New York—Intellectual life—Juvenile literature. 7. African American
arts—New York (State)—New York—History—20th century—Juvenile
literature. 8. New York (N.Y.)—Intellectual life—20th century—Juvenile
literature. I. Title.
  E185.6.K253 2009
  305.896´07307471—dc22
                                                                    2008051299

Lucent Books
27500 Drake Rd.
Farmington Hills, MI 48331

ISBN-13: 978-1-4205-0104-9
ISBN-10: 1-4205-0104-6

Contents

Foreword

The United States has existed as a nation for over 200 years. By comparison, Rome existed as a nation-state for more than 1,000 years. Out of a few struggling British colonies, the United States developed relatively quickly into a world power whose policy decisions and culture have great influence on the world stage. What events and aspirations drove this young American nation to such great heights in such a short period of time? The answer lies in a close study of its varied and unique history. As author James Baldwin once remarked, "American history is longer, larger, more various, more beautiful, and more terrible than anything anyone has ever said about it."

The basic facts of U.S. history—names, dates, places, battles, treaties, speeches, and acts of Congress—fill countless textbooks. These facts, though essential to a thorough understanding of world events, are rarely compelling for students. More compelling are the stories in history, the experience of history.

Titles in the American History series explore the history of a country and the experiences of its people. What influences led the colonists to risk everything and break from Britain? Who was the driving force behind the Constitution? What factors led thousands of people to leave their homelands and settle in the United States? Questions like these do not have simple answers; by discussing them, however, we can view the past as a more real, interesting, and accessible place.

Students will find excellent tools for research and investigation in every title. Lucent Books' American History series provides not only facts, but also the analysis and context necessary for insightful critical thinking about history and about current events. Fully cited quotations from historical figures, eyewitnesses, letters, speeches, and writings bring vibrancy and authority to the text. Annotated bibliographies allow students to evaluate and locate sources for further investigation. Sidebars highlight important and interesting figures, events, or related primary source excerpts. Timelines, maps, and full-color images add another dimension of accessibility to the stories being told.

It has been said that the past has a history of repeating itself, for good and ill. In these pages, students will learn a bit about both and, perhaps, better understand their own place in this world.

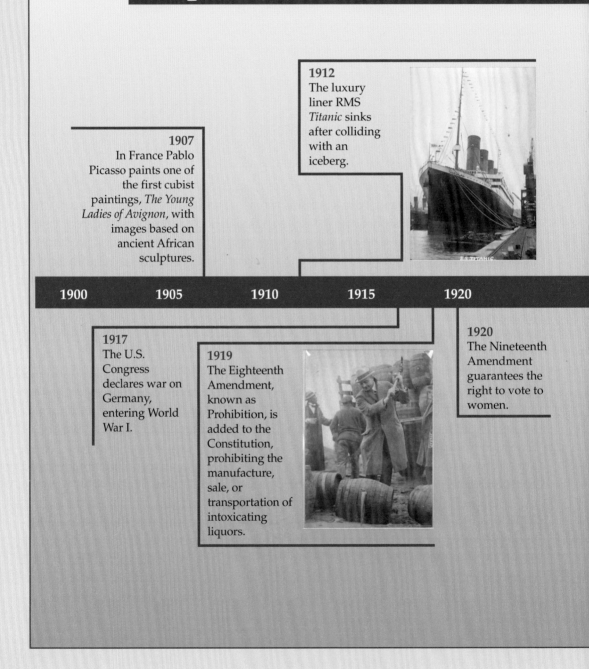

1907
In France Pablo Picasso paints one of the first cubist paintings, *The Young Ladies of Avignon*, with images based on ancient African sculptures.

1912
The luxury liner RMS *Titanic* sinks after colliding with an iceberg.

1900   1905   1910   1915   1920

1917
The U.S. Congress declares war on Germany, entering World War I.

1919
The Eighteenth Amendment, known as Prohibition, is added to the Constitution, prohibiting the manufacture, sale, or transportation of intoxicating liquors.

1920
The Nineteenth Amendment guarantees the right to vote to women.

the Harlem Renaissance

1929
The Great Depression begins with the U.S. stock market crash of "Black Thursday," October 24th. A worldwide economic depression ensues.

1931
The 102-story Empire State Building opens in New York City.

1925
The trial of John Scopes begins, causing controversy over the teaching of Charles Darwin's theory of evolution in schools.

| 1925 | 1930 | 1935 | 1940 |

1933
The Eighteenth Amendment, Prohibition, is repealed.

1936
Jesse Owens wins four gold medals at the Olympic Games in Berlin, Germany.

1927
Charles Lindbergh completes first nonstop solo flight across the Atlantic Ocean.

1928
Amelia Earhart becomes the first woman to fly across the Atlantic Ocean.

A Rebirth of Black Culture

The word *renaissance* comes from the French word for rebirth, and in the 1920s, African American culture was reborn in Harlem, a neighborhood in New York, New York. The Harlem Renaissance took place nearly three hundred years after the first Africans were brought to New York as slaves—and more than a half century after President Abraham Lincoln ended slavery.

The Harlem Renaissance was a great awakening that redefined the black urban experience. It was led by young African American writers, playwrights, actors, singers, artists, intellectuals, and jazz and blues musicians. They came from many backgrounds, most were not even from Harlem, and they were not always connected by similar beliefs concerning art, politics, or society. But contributors to the renaissance shared a common goal. They wanted to provide a unifying voice for the 10 million members of a segregated black population struggling to coexist with about 80 million white people living in the United States.

The Great Migration

The renaissance that shook Harlem, and the white world beyond, began at the end of World War I in 1918 and tapered off in the 1930s. However, the renaissance had roots in the nineteenth century, and many aspects of the reawakening stretched into the 1950s and 1960s.

There were many issues at work that provided an environment for the growth of the Harlem Renaissance. During the first decades of the twentieth century, African Americans still struggled with extreme poverty, racism, segregation, and institutional violence in nearly every city and state in the United States.

Black people were prevented from working in good jobs, from buying

A Ku Klux Klan rally in West Virginia in 1924. The KKK terrorized the black community to prevent them from exercising their civil rights.

homes, and from attending decent schools. Most black people lived in segregated neighborhoods where they patronized black-owned restaurants, theaters, clothing shops, and taverns. But African Americans were largely barred from public spaces, including swimming pools, parks, and restrooms. They were expected to keep to themselves and avoid mingling with white society.

Things were particularly bad for blacks living in the Deep South and in rural areas of Indiana and other states in the Midwest. The vigilante group Ku Klux Klan (KKK) was a powerful force in many states. Mayors, police chiefs, and even state legislators and governors were among its millions of members. The KKK terrorized black communities and lynched countless African Americans to prevent them from exercising their civil rights.

This terrorism, coupled with poor economic conditions and race riots in many cities, led Southern blacks to uproot their lives. In what is called the Great Migration, millions of African Americans moved to industrial cities in the North, such as New York, where there was a greater degree of freedom and opportunity.

Paul Lawrence Dunbar's 1902 book, The Sport of the Gods, *was the first novel about black life in New York City.*

Like Heaven

The working-class blacks brought their unique cultural mix to their new urban settings. Notable African American contributions to society include blues and jazz music, which first emerged in the racism and poverty of New Orleans, Louisiana, before traveling up the Mississippi River and spreading east to Chicago, Illinois, and New York. In the world of literature, authors such as Paul Laurence Dunbar, whose parents had been slaves, achieved fame writing about southern black life in the poetic dialect of southern African Americans. Dunbar's 1902 book, *The Sport of the Gods*, was the first novel about black life in New York City. In it Dunbar describes the mythical status the city held in the imaginations of poor black southerners:

> [They] had heard of New York as a place vague and far away, a city that, like Heaven, to them had existed by faith alone. All the days of their lives they had heard about it, and it seemed to them the center of all the glory, all the wealth, and all the freedom of the world.[1]

Like European immigrants who had heard the streets of New York were paved with gold, the reality of the city may have disappointed some of the African Americans who moved there. Unskilled black women living in Harlem labored as maids, dressmakers, beauticians, and cooks. Men were hired as elevator operators, shoe shiners, porters, doormen, messengers, waiters, janitors, and day laborers. However, even these jobs presented better opportunities than those in the South. And unlike most of the South, Harlem had its share of black shop and restaurant owners as well as professionals, including lawyers, doctors, nurses, teachers, and preachers.

A Teeming, Overcrowded Ghetto

While a few business owners, landlords, and creative individuals did well for themselves, the majority of Harlem residents remained poor before, during, and after the renaissance. However, the mix of old and new cultures, from the Deep South, New York City, and even the Caribbean, provided artistic inspiration for the creative people behind the Harlem Renaissance. As history professor Cary D. Wintz states in *Black Culture and the Harlem Renaissance*,

> [The neighborhood] provided the material and the setting for many literary creations of the Renaissance. The poetry, short stories, and novels of the period abound with scenes and characters lifted from Harlem's streets and cabarets.… Harlem though … was a teeming, overcrowded ghetto, and much of its laughter and gaiety only thinly veiled the misery and poverty that was becoming the standard of life for the new black urban masses. This, too, was reflected by the Harlem Renaissance.[2]

What made the era so unique was the fact that it was not only black people celebrating their culture in what was called the "The World's Greatest Negro Metropolis." White people were also learning about the joys and troubles, the elation and degradations of life for African Americans.

The Harlem Renaissance was one of the first times that black and white people read the same literature, attended theater together, danced together, and sang together. It was a brief period, however, and racism was still rampant among white participants, many of whom described their trips to Harlem as "slumming." But for those in New York's African American community, the renaissance proved to be a celebration of pride, culture, black identity, and black history. For the first time, the achievements of black people were visible for all to see. And after three centuries of racism, slavery, and prejudice, African Americans ceased being invisible in the land of their birth.

Chapter One

The New Negro Movement

Harlem occupies less than 2 square miles (5 sq. km) of Manhattan Island in the northern, or uptown, area of New York City. In 1925 the neighborhood was home to more than 150,000 black people, a melting pot of African Americans from New York and the South as well as immigrants from Jamaica, Haiti, Cuba, Puerto Rico, and Africa. But at that time Harlem had only been the center of black urban culture in the United States for about fifteen years. The story of its transformation to "The World's Greatest Negro Metropolis" can be traced to a convergence of capitalism, poverty, opportunity, and racism.

Historian Leon Litwack describes the early decades of the twentieth century as "the most violent and repressive period in the history of race relations in the United States."[3] This was especially true in Virginia, Louisiana, Alabama, Mississippi, Georgia, and the Carolinas, where 80 percent of black Americans lived in rural areas in 1900. Most worked as sharecroppers, farming land owned by others for a small percentage of the crops. Sharecroppers were the poorest of the poor, working long hours but wearing rags, living in tiny shacks, and suffering from malnutrition and a host of diseases.

Between 1910 and 1920, there was a steady exodus from the terrible conditions in the rural South. About 1.5 million African Americans moved north to urban ghettos in cities such as Chicago, Detroit, Cleveland, and Philadelphia. The movement, known as the Great Migration, completely changed the face of Manhattan. The black population of Harlem doubled from 50,000 in 1914 to over 100,000 in 1920. Of these black New Yorkers, about a quarter were natives of the city, another quarter were foreign born, and about half were from other states, principally in the South. Another 50,000 blacks migrated to the city between 1920 and 1925. By 1930, the African

American population of Harlem was over well 200,000. (The population of New York City itself was about 5.6 million in 1920.)

The center of this population explosion occurred between 125th Street on the south and 155th Street to the north, bordered on the west by Morningside Drive and on the east by the East River—the neighborhood known as Harlem.

The "Negro Invasion"

Harlem was virtually all white in 1901 when a bitter dispute broke out between two landlords in neighboring houses. Although the cause of the disagreement is unknown, one landlord rented his building out to black tenants in order to anger his rival. The landlord turned the task over to Philip A. Payton Jr., a porter who was desperately struggling to become Manhattan's first African American real estate agent. Payton had no problem finding tenants—there was an extreme housing shortage for black people in Manhattan because few landlords would rent to minorities. Payton managed the property and was able to convince other landlords into letting him manage their houses and apartments.

In 1903 Payton was so successful he was able to spend five hundred thousand

Harlem had a population boom during the first part of the twentieth century as African Americans left the South for the promise of a better life in the North. Pictured here is 125th Street in Harlem in 1935.

dollars (equal to 12 million dollars in 2008), to start the Afro-American Realty Company in downtown Manhattan. Within a few years, Payton was known as "the father of black Harlem," having changed the racial character of the neighborhood almost single-handedly. Payton's company failed in 1908, but by that time other black real estate agents were following in his footsteps. This resulted not only in black people moving into apartment houses but also purchasing houses in the neighborhood.

Not everyone was happy with Harlem's black migration. White people were in a panic, fleeing in droves from what they called the "Negro Invasion." As author and educator James Weldon Johnson described it in 1927,

In the eyes of the whites who were antagonistic, the whole movement

"A City Within a City"

Author, educator, and early civil rights activist James Weldon Johnson was one of the leading literary voices of the Harlem Renaissance. Writing for Survey Graphic *magazine in March 1925, Johnson describes Harlem:*

In the make-up of New York, Harlem is not merely a Negro colony or community, it is a city within a city, the greatest Negro city in the world. It is not a slum or a fringe, it is located in the heart of Manhattan and occupies one of the most beautiful and healthful sections of the city. It is not a "quarter" of dilapidated tenements, but is made up of [new] apartments and handsome dwellings, with well-paved and well-lighted streets. It has its own churches, social and civic centers, shops, theatres and other places of amusement. And it contains more Negroes to the square mile than any other spot on earth. A stranger who rides up magnificent Seventh Avenue on a bus or in an automobile must be struck with surprise at the transformation which takes place after he crosses One Hundred and Twenty-fifth Street. Beginning there, the population suddenly darkens and he rides through twenty-five solid blocks where the passers-by, the shoppers, those sitting in restaurants, coming out of theatres, standing in doorways and looking out of windows are practically all Negroes…. There is nothing just like it in any other city in the country, for there is no preparation for it; no change in the character of the houses and streets; no change, indeed, in the appearance of the people, except their color.

James Weldon Johnson, "The Making of Harlem," *Survey Graphic*, March 1925, http://etext.virginia.edu/harlem/JohMakiF.html.

took on the aspect of an "invasion"—an invasion of both their economic and their social rights. They felt that Negroes as neighbors not only lowered the values of their property, but also lowered their social status…. Their conduct could be compared to that of a community in the Middle Ages fleeing before an epidemic of the black plague…. The presence of a single colored family in a block, regardless of the fact that they might be well-bred people, with sufficient means to buy their new home, was a signal for precipitate [hasty] flight. The stampeded whites actually deserted house after house and block after block.[4]

For once, racism benefited the black community, as they were able to purchase or rent the vacated properties. By 1911 African Americans had purchased 10 percent of Harlem's large apartment buildings, called tenements, and 40 percent of its private homes. As black real estate agent John Royall stated, "the colored people are in Harlem to stay."[5]

Harlem Is Practically Owned by Negroes

Even as real estate prices were falling, the economic picture was improving for many people living in Harlem. In 1914 World War I broke out in Europe. Even before the United States joined the fight and declared war on Germany in April 1917, the government was active in aiding its allies in Europe. Wartime industries were under orders to produce a record number of armaments, clothes, rations, and other goods. At the same time, the war cut off the steady supply of white laborers that had been immigrating from Europe to New York since the 1880s. This created a labor shortage, and employers began to hire African Americans. This attracted even more blacks from the rural South.

For the first time, black laborers were making good wages, saving money, and investing in real estate. By 1920 it was not unusual for an African American family to walk into a real estate office and put down anywhere from one to five thousand dollars in cash to purchase property.

Some of the stories of black entrepreneurs making fortunes in real estate are legendary, such as the one James Weldon Johnson published in 1925 about Mary Dean. Known as "Pig Foot Mary," she was able to achieve success by selling "soul food," such as fried chicken and pickled pig's feet, from a small stand in Harlem. Johnson writes:

> "Pig Foot Mary" is a character in Harlem. Everybody who knows the corner of Lenox Avenue and One Hundred and Thirty-fifth Street knows "Mary" and her stand and has been tempted by the smell of her pigsfeet fried chicken and hot corn, even if he has not been a customer. "Mary" … bought the five-story apartment house at the corner

African Americans were able to buy property and own their own businesses in record numbers in Harlem.

of Seventh Avenue and One Hundred and Thirty-seventh Street at a price of $42,000. Later she sold it to the Y.W.C.A. for dormitory purposes ... [for] $72,000.[6]

Dozens of success stories of this type abounded in the neighborhood and the total value of property owned by blacks in Harlem in 1925 exceeded 60 million dollars. And the buying and selling created some of the first black real estate moguls in New York history, as Johnson writes:

[This] is amazing, especially when we take into account the short time in which [it happened]. Twenty years ago Negroes were begging for the privilege of renting a flat in Harlem. Fifteen years ago barely a half dozen colored men owned real property in all Manhattan. And down to ten years ago the amount that had been acquired in Harlem was comparatively negligible. Today [1925] Negro Harlem is practically owned by Negroes.[7]

A New Dignity

With poverty rates falling and property ownership on the upswing, the stage was set for a cultural rebirth in Harlem. All that was needed was a trigger to set the renaissance in motion. And many believe that the catalyst of the New Negro movement was a victory parade that took place on February 17, 1919, several months after the end of World War I. On that sunny winter morning, thirteen hundred veterans of the all-black 369th Infantry Regiment marched up Fifth Avenue along with their military jazz band.

The infantry, named the "Hellfighters" by the French, was made up of the first black troops sent to fight on the European battlefront in World War I. They spent 191 continuous days engaged in trench warfare, and their valor was legendary on both sides of the conflict. While the German enemy called them the *Blutlustige Schwarze Männer*, or "bloodthirsty black men," the French called them heroes for saving France.

Wounded soldiers of the 369th Infantry Regiment, known as the "Harlem Hellfighters," took part in a parade in New York City, celebrating the return of World War I soldiers, in 1919. Some credit the event with sparking the New Negro Renaissance.

The 369th was the only American unit awarded the Croix de Guerre, the French High Command's highest mark of honor.

The marching Harlem Hellfighters were led by the regiment's sixty-piece band under the direction of Lieutenant James Reese Europe. Big Jim Europe had been a legendary trumpeter before the war and just as the Hellfighters beat the German enemy, Big Jim's jazzy music conquered audiences in France, Belgium, and England. But on that spectacular February morning, hundreds of thousands of adoring Americans stood in the streets or waved flags from office windows as the Hellfighters marched with military precision up Fifth Avenue.

The white audiences downtown applauded politely for the black soldiers, but after they crossed over to Lenox and entered Harlem they received a heroes' welcome. Girlfriends and relatives joined the ranks of soldiers while a torrent of pennants, flags, banners, and scarves rained down on the men. According to the newspaper *New York Age,*

> Never in the history of [New York] has such a rousing royal welcome been given returning heroes from the field of battle; not for many a day is it likely that thousands ... of colored citizens will participate in such a tumultuous and enthusiastic demonstration.... [In] Harlem the greeting bordered on riot.... Playing "Here Comes My Daddy Now," the Hellfighters marched between two howling walls of humanity.

Those unable to secure standing room on the sidewalk hung from windows and lampposts, while from the rooftops thousands stood and whooped things up.[8]

The Harlem Hellfighters were among 380,000 African Americans who served during World War I. But the soldiers faced severe discrimination and were segregated within the military. After spending time in France, the black soldiers discovered that they had more rights in Europe than they did in the United States. In the Chicago African American newspaper *Defender* in 1919 Lieutenant William N. Colson writes, "While in France, the Negro soldiers ... discovered that the only white men that treated them as men were native Europeans, and especially the French with their wider social experience and finer social sense. The Frenchman was unable to comprehend American color prejudice. The Englishman was much more democratic than the American."[9]

This fair treatment helped the heroes of Harlem return home with a new sense of dignity. They were done cowering under the bludgeon of white racism and were willing to take risks to prove their worth to a society that had never valued their contributions. The New Negro movement had begun in Harlem.

The Next War for Democracy

Black veterans were among the most eager to fight for equal rights after the war. However, there was a political divide within the African American community.

Black World War I veterans came home determined to fight against discrimination and injustice in the United States. Here, marchers take part in an anti-lynching parade in Harlem in 1919.

On one side older black leaders such as William Edward Burghardt (W.E.B.) Du Bois, founder of the National Association for the Advancement of Colored People (NAACP), worked with white supporters who believed that nonviolence was the path to equal rights and integration. Some felt his efforts were geared toward helping the small number of middle-class blacks and professionals, rather than the poor, uneducated masses. This alienated young black radicals who called themselves "New Negroes" as a way to distinguish themselves from traditional leaders. The New Negroes did not necessarily believe in integration and many believed that violence was the only solution to their problems. This new posture was clearly defined by Oklahoma publisher Roscoe Dunjee, writing in the newspaper *Black Dispatch*: "The New Negro, who stands today released in spirit, finds himself, in America ... physically bound and shackled by LAWS AND CUSTOMS THAT WERE MADE FOR SLAVES, and all of the unrest ... charged to my people IS THE BATTLE OF FREE MEN POUNDING ON WALLS THAT SURROUND THEM."[10]

His Excellency

The UNIA held its first convention in Harlem in August 1920. Marcus Garvey used the occasion to have himself named His Excellency the Provisional President of Africa. An article in New York Age, *quoted in* This Was Harlem, *describes the induction ceremony:*

[U]pon] the arrival of His Excellency the Provisional President, the band played the [UNIA's] national anthem of Africa—then His Excellency, whose garb was topped by a towering red plume, ascended the kingly dais, followed by a procession of subjects passing in review, led by the Chaplin General and other officials.

Deputies and a number of delegates, men and women, were presented to His Excellency, and each one was required to kneel in humble submission at the foot of the throne.

The individuals chosen for special high honors were announced as having been recommended by His Excellency the President.... The honors dispensed included "Duke of Uganda," "Duke of the Niger," "Knight Commander, Order of the Nile," and "Knight Commander, Distinguished Service Order of Ethiopia."

The subjects honored were brought to the foot of the throne, where each kneeled and received his accolade from the sword wielded by His Excellency.

Quoted in Jervis Anderson, *This Was Harlem.* New York: Farrar Straus Giroux, 1982, p. 125.

Many of those Dunjee identified as New Negroes supported black nationalist and black liberation movements that struck fear in the hearts of the white establishment. Black nationalists believed African Americans should be proud of their heritage and advocated building separate communities based on black pride. Black war veterans, who were leading members of the New Negro movement, were ready to fight back against the KKK and other vigilantes who were lynching African Americans on a regular basis in the South. Colson summed up the feelings of many when

he wrote, "The next war for democracy [will] be in the land of 'THE STAR SPANGLED BANNER.'"[11]

Marcus Garvey's Black Nationalism

The indisputable leader of the New Negro movement was not a war veteran or a southerner but a Jamaican immigrant. Marcus Garvey moved to the United States in 1916 and set up the headquarters of the Universal Negro Improvement Association (UNIA) in Harlem in 1917. The organization started with thirteen members, including Garvey, but

Marcus Garvey was the leader of the Universal Negro Improvement Association (UNIA). He believed all blacks should move to Africa and start their own free nation.

quickly grew beyond the borders of Harlem. Garvey preached a "Back to Africa" or Pan-African message, calling for all black people to move to Africa and start their own free nation.

Any person of African descent could join UNIA for thirty-five cents and a pledge to support the association. Within months of its founding, the UNIA swelled to twelve thousand members and by 1918, the organization's influential *Negro World* newspaper had a circulation of five hundred thousand. In 1920 Garvey claimed there were 2 million UNIA members in the United States, Central and South America, and the Caribbean. While experts believe Garvey inflated the membership numbers, there is little doubt that the UNIA had a powerful influence in Harlem where about one out of every three residents belonged to the organization.

Taking advantage of his widespread support, Garvey planned several money-making projects to pay for his dream of founding an independent black nation. And in doing so, he was able to promote black nationalism by providing employment and economic independence through several successful business ventures in Harlem. These businesses, which were staffed and run by blacks, were part of the Negro Factories Corporation (NFC), founded in 1919.

The corporation was financed by donations raised through *Negro World* and with a stock offering Garvey said would be used to "build and operate factories in the big industrial centers of the United States, Central America, the West Indies, and Africa to manufacture every marketable commodity."[12] To this end the NFC established the Universal Laundries, the Universal Millinery Store, Universal Restaurants, Universal Grocery Stores, a hotel, a tailoring business, a printer, and a factory which made African American dolls.

Within months, the NFC became a symbol of African American business expertise in Harlem. The company's grocery stores and restaurants competed successfully with white-owned businesses by offering foods from the Caribbean, the American South, and Africa. Meanwhile, Garvey's Universal Steam and Electric Laundry was considered the best laundry in Harlem. The UNIA also ran the Men's Manufacturing Department and the Women's Manufacturing Department which produced Panama hats, shirts, ties, dresses, undergarments, and other clothes. And the offices of the corporation provided employment that Harlem residents were denied elsewhere. Hundreds of men and women found work as managers, clerks, accountants, stenographers, and secretaries. In addition, women, who made up half the UNIA membership, were often put in positions of authority. This was considered quite unusual during an era when men dominated business and politics.

The NFC also invested in real estate, offices, and empty factories that were rented at a discount to faltering black-owned businesses. Garvey considered their success important to the black

Women in the UNIA

Throughout its existence, the membership of the UNIA was about 50 percent women. On the American Experience Web site, civil rights activist and author Barbara Blair discusses how the organization and its founder, Marcus Garvey, empowered black women in ways that were unique in American culture in the 1920s:

Garvey lauded the women in the movement. He recognized their importance as loyal supporters, and he idealized them—in his speeches, editorials, songs and poems,—in ways [that fit] with the larger message of black pride of the movement, and in sharp and welcome contrast to the negative white stereotypes that demeaned and degraded black femininity. The UNIA as a whole heralded the importance of black motherhood and the nurturing of black children, in part as a remedy and counter balance to the violence, repression, poverty and racism faced in daily lives. They also took very seriously the political contribution of women raising and educating black children to pride and knowledge of the history of their race.

Many women embraced these roles and images, including the idea of black women as beautiful and the centrality and worth of motherhood…. But they also wanted more…. Over time, many Garveyite women … called on each other to, if necessary, sweep ineffectual men aside and take the reins of leadership into their own hands.

Barbara Blair, "Online Forum: Comparing the Role of Women in the Garvey Movement," American Experience, 2000, www.pbs.org/wgbh/amex/garvey/sfeature/sf_forum_14.html.

independence movement. In 1920 he wrote,

All these [financial achievements] to the ordinary optimist would seem a miracle, but all these things have been accomplished through the determination of the men and women who banded themselves together as members of the movement. Wherever there is a will there is a way, and the will of the New Negro is to do or die.[13]

The Negro Moses

Nowhere was the New Negro movement more on display than the first UNIA convention held in Harlem in August 1920. The boisterous event attracted twenty-five thousand members who named Garvey "His Excellency the Provisional President of Africa." In this role he claimed to represent the African government in exile and act as leader of all black people throughout the world. Garvey created his own Harlem royalty, bestowing titles, such as Duke of the Nile and

Thousands taking part in the annual parade of the Universal Negro Improvement Association in Harlem in 1920.

Viscount of Niger, on his closest advisers. Bearers of these titles—and Garvey himself—appeared in gaudy military-style uniforms bedecked with medals and decorations, all tailor-made by the NFC. The UNIA also adopted a national flag—a red, black, and green banner said to represent the motherland, Africa.

After the opening ceremonies, the UNIA convention hosted a three-hour parade through Harlem that was grander than the one that welcomed the return of the Hellfighters. The uniformed African royalty led fifty thousand UNIA members in a pageant that stretched for ten city blocks. Garvey was the central focus, regally seated in a Packard convertible wearing a purple, green, and black uniform festooned with gold braids and a hat with red plumes. Supporters carried signs that read "Garvey the Negro Moses—Long May He Live" and "The Negro Fought in Europe, He Can Fight in Africa."[14]

Garvey's Critics

The pomp, ceremony, and public adulation frightened traditional African American leaders who disparaged Garvey's combination of politics and self-promotion. Du Bois was especially critical calling Garvey a "little fat black man, ugly … with a big head,"[15] and noting that some had invested their entire life savings in Garvey's various stock market offerings. In a 1921 article in *Crisis*, the newspaper of the NAACP, quoted in *Voices of a Black Nation*, Du Bois writes:

[Garvey is] a stubborn, domineering leader of the masses; he has worthy industrial and commercial schemes but he is an inexperienced business man. His ... methods are bombastic, wasteful, illogical and ineffective and almost illegal.[16]

Du Bois was not the only person examining the business practices of the UNIA. Garvey's Pan-African message frightened many within the U.S. government who feared a violent black uprising. The Federal Bureau of Investigation (FBI), the State Department, the U.S. Postal Service, and even military intelligence agents used the threat as an excuse to spy on Garvey, break into his offices, and infiltrate the UNIA. One of the officials in the campaign to stop Garvey, Postmaster General Roger A. Bowen, summed up the perceived threat, saying the UNIA leader intended "to instill into the minds of negroes ... that they have been greatly wronged and oppressed by the white races and that they can only hope for relief and redress through concerted and aggressive action on their part."[17]

In 1922 Garvey was formally charged with using the U.S. Postal Service to defraud buyers of UNIA stock. He was convicted and imprisoned in a federal penitentiary in Atlanta, Georgia. Upon his release in 1927, Garvey was deported to Jamaica where he died in obscurity in 1940.

Garvey spent much of the Harlem Renaissance fighting what some saw as prejudicial persecution by the U.S. government. After Garvey went to jail, his wife, Amy Jacques Garvey, kept UNIA alive, and the group's philosophies provided a strong political foundation for the Harlem Renaissance. By promoting racial consciousness and a powerful sense of independence and black pride, Garvey provided hope in a time of despair. And his message inspired the writers, artists, and musicians of the Harlem Renaissance.

Chapter Two

The Literary Crowd

During the 1920s, the Harlem Renaissance was often referred to as the Negro Literary Renaissance by the writers, poets, and intellectuals who were at the center of the movement. While jazz, art, and musical theater played important roles in the renaissance, the intellectual basis for the movement was formulated among the writers. These men and women were the leaders of Harlem's so-called Talented Tenth, the 10 percent of the neighborhood residents that were successful doctors, lawyers, publishers, musicians, actors, and authors.

The writers of the Negro Literary Renaissance were keenly aware that they were creating a closely examined literary movement. This self-consciousness led them to strictly define the movement's boundaries in order to further their goals, which included increasing interest in black history and culture and promoting racial pride.

The promoters of the Harlem Renaissance were inspired by a previous generation who wrote about their African heritage and black American folk culture in the late 1890s. For example, the American Negro Academy (ANA), founded in Washington, D.C., in 1897, brought together black intellectuals who promoted African American literature, arts, music, and history.

As an outgrowth of their work, by the 1910s, there were at least five hundred newspapers and magazines in the United States devoted to black social, historical, and cultural issues. And in 1915, Carter Woodson, a Harvard PhD, founded the Association for the Study of Negro Life and History, the first black historical association. This organization publishes the *Journal of African American History* (originally named the *Journal of Negro History*) and promotes Black History Month, which is now celebrated in the United States and Canada.

Carter Woodson founded the Association for the Study of Negro Life and History, the first black historical association.

Two Souls, Two Thoughts

W.E.B. Du Bois was among the scholars who wrote papers for the ANA in its early years, and his 1903 book, *The Souls of Black Folk*, was extremely influential. In the book Du Bois puts forth the idea that African Americans are torn between two conflicting worlds, their African heritage and their American homeland:

> [The] Negro is … born with a veil, and gifted with second-sight in this American world,—a world which yields him no true self-consciousness, but only lets him see himself through the revelation of the [American] world. It is a peculiar sensation, this double-consciousness, this sense of always looking at one's self through the eyes of others, of measuring one's soul by the tape of a world that looks on in amused contempt and pity. One ever feels his two-ness,—an American, a Negro; two souls, two thoughts, two unreconciled strivings; two warring ideals in one dark body, whose dogged strength alone keeps it from being torn asunder.[18]

Harlem Renaissance writers Langston Hughes and James Weldon Johnson both credited *The Souls of Black Folk* for providing inspiration to them in their early years. Hughes said it was "my earliest memory of any book except a schoolbook,"[19] while Johnson said it was "a work which … has had a greater effect

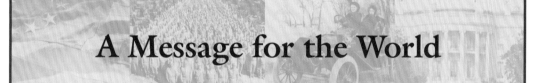

A Message for the World

The Souls of Black Folk, *written in 1903 by W.E.B. Du Bois, was extremely influential among the writers of the Harlem Renaissance. In the excerpt below, Du Bois examines what it's like to be both a Negro and an American:*

The history of the American Negro is the history of this strife,—this longing to attain self-conscious manhood, to merge his double self into a better and truer self. In this merging he wishes neither of the older selves to be lost. He would not Africanize America, for America has too much to teach the world and Africa. He would not bleach his Negro soul in a flood of white Americanism, for he knows that Negro blood has a message for the world. He simply wishes to make it possible for a man to be both a Negro and an American, without being cursed and spit upon by his fellows, without having the doors of opportunity closed roughly in his face.

W.E.B. Du Bois, *The Souls of Black Folk*. Chicago: McClurg, 1903, www.bartleby.com/114 /1.html.

upon and within the Negro race in America than any other single [book] published."[20]

"Icy Cold, and White Hot"

When poet Claude McKay read *The Souls of Black Folk* in 1912, he said "it shook me like an earthquake."[21] Born in Jamaica, McKay too felt that he was torn between his African roots and the traditions of the whites that ruled his native land. Living in Harlem in 1919, McKay was among the first poets to encapsulate the experiences of the black urban masses. He wrote "If We Must Die" during the Red Summer of 1919, when twenty-five race riots

Poet Claude McKay was among the first poets to describe the experiences of African Americans in his writing.

occurred in major American cities including Charleston; Washington, D.C.; and Chicago. The riots were largely attacks on black neighborhoods by unemployed whites who were angry that African Americans had taken many factory jobs. During Red Summer, forty-three black men were lynched, eight were burned at the stake, and hundreds died from other racial violence.

"If We Must Die" calls for aggressive self-defense against the rioters. A few of the lines read:

> If we must die, let it not be like hogs
> Hunted and penned in an inglorious spot,
> While round us bark the mad and hungry dogs,

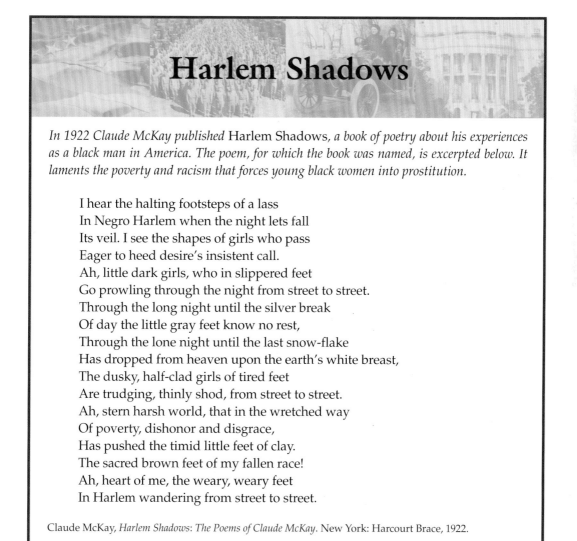

Harlem Shadows

In 1922 Claude McKay published Harlem Shadows, *a book of poetry about his experiences as a black man in America. The poem, for which the book was named, is excerpted below. It laments the poverty and racism that forces young black women into prostitution.*

I hear the halting footsteps of a lass
In Negro Harlem when the night lets fall
Its veil. I see the shapes of girls who pass
Eager to heed desire's insistent call.
Ah, little dark girls, who in slippered feet
Go prowling through the night from street to street.
Through the long night until the silver break
Of day the little gray feet know no rest,
Through the lone night until the last snow-flake
Has dropped from heaven upon the earth's white breast,
The dusky, half-clad girls of tired feet
Are trudging, thinly shod, from street to street.
Ah, stern harsh world, that in the wretched way
Of poverty, dishonor and disgrace,
Has pushed the timid little feet of clay.
The sacred brown feet of my fallen race!
Ah, heart of me, the weary, weary feet
In Harlem wandering from street to street.

Claude McKay, *Harlem Shadows: The Poems of Claude McKay*. New York: Harcourt Brace, 1922.

Making their mock at our accursed
   lot....
O kinsmen we must meet the common foe!
Though far outnumbered let us
   show us brave,
And for their thousand blows deal
   one deathblow!
What though before us lies the open
   grave?
Like men we'll face the murderous,
   cowardly pack,
Pressed to the wall, dying, but fighting back![22]

McKay, who was thirty at the time the
poem was published, expressed similar
sentiments in poems such as "America,"
"The White City," "In Bondage," "En-
slaved," "Outcast," and "The Lynching."
These appeared in McKay's 1922 book
Harlem Shadows along with more than
sixty other poems.

With the publication of *Harlem Shadows*,
McKay became the most celebrated black
poet in the United States. In the *New Repub-
lic* magazine, white critic Robert Littel discusses *Harlem Shadows* and mentions the
talents of James Weldon Johnson. Little
concludes that the two authors "make me
sit up and take notice when they write
about their race and ours. They strike hard
and pierce deep. It is not merely poetic
emotions they express, but something fierce
and constant, icy cold, and white hot."[23]

Lift Every Voice

By the time Littel made those comments,
James Weldon Johnson was one of the
most successful African Americans in

the United States. Born in 1871, he had
enrolled in the all-black Atlanta University at the age of sixteen and in 1897 he
was the first African American to take
the Florida Bar Exam to become a lawyer. But the segregation in the South
weighed heavily on Johnson so he began writing song lyrics with his brother
Rosamond. They traveled to New York
in 1899 to sell their work, and within a
few years the Johnson brothers were a
successful songwriting team. Songs
such as "The Congo Love Song" and
"Under the Bamboo Tree" were so popular that people bought hundreds of
thousands of copies of the sheet music,
making the Johnsons wealthy men. But
the song "Lift Every Voice and Sing,"
about liberty bringing a new day after
the dark night of slavery, was an instant
classic. Written in 1900 to commemorate
the anniversary of President Abraham
Lincoln's birthday, the song became
known as the Negro National Anthem
and is still widely sung today.

In 1912 Johnson penned the novel *The
Autobiography of an Ex-Colored Man* about
a light-skinned African American who
passes himself off as white, marries a white
woman, and has two children. The plot
was extremely controversial for the time
and Johnson published it anonymously.

Like the conflicted subjects of *The
Souls of Black Folk*, the protagonist in *Ex-
Colored Man* is filled with self-doubt
about his identity as an African American. He rejects his blackness after wit-
nessing a vicious lynching, shamed that
he belonged to a race that could be
treated in such a manner. However,

after reading books by Frederick Douglass and other black luminaries, the protagonist comes to appreciate black folk culture with its musical and storytelling traditions. The plot takes an autobiographical turn when the character, like Johnson, becomes a composer and ragtime piano player, writing songs that blend American music with black spiritual traditions in order to present a positive image of African Americans to the world.

The Measure of Greatness

Although *The Autobiography of an Ex-Colored Man* only found a small audience when it was published, Johnson continued to write fiction, nonfiction, and poetry. He was also editor of the newspaper *New York Age*, where he wrote the influential "Views and Reviews" column between 1915 and 1923. During this period, Johnson published *The Book of American Negro Poetry*, with the words of thirty-one black poets, most of whom were

"The Dilemma of the Negro Author"

Several black writers of the Harlem Renaissance became quite popular in the 1920s. But their books were published by the white New York literary establishment for white audiences. Therefore African American authors had to consider the racial prejudices of their white readers in order to be successful. In his 1928 essay, "The Dilemma of the Negro Author," James Weldon Johnson explains the problems:

If the Negro author selects white America as his audience, he is bound to run up against … a whole row of hard-set stereotypes which are not easily broken up. White America has some firm opinions as to what the Negro is, and consequently some pretty well fixed ideas as to what should be written about him, and how.

What is the Negro in the artistic conception of white America? In the brighter light, he is a simple, indolent, docile, improvident peasant; a singing, dancing, laughing weeping child; picturesque beside his log cabin and in the snowy fields of cotton; naïvely charming with his banjo and his songs in the moonlight and along the lazy Southern rivers; a faithful, ever-smiling and genuflecting old servitor to the white folks of quality; a pathetic and pitiable figure.… Ninety-nine one-hundredths of all that has been written about the Negro in the United States in three centuries and read with any degree of interest or pleasure by white America has been written in conformity to one or more of these ideas.

James Weldon Johnson, "The Dilemma of the Negro Author," in *The Harlem Renaissance 1920–1940*, vol. 2, *The Politics and Aesthetics of "New Negro" Literature*, ed. Cary D. Wintz. New York: Garland, 1996, p. 248.

Although he was a successful lawyer, James Weldon Johnson became best known as an accomplished writer.

unknown. In the preface to the book Johnson states that stereotypes of African American inferiority could be easily disproved if people were only aware of the contributions black people have made to the arts. He says:

> The public, generally speaking, does not know that there are American Negro poets.... It is a matter which has a direct bearing on the most vital of American problems. A people may become great through many means, but there is only one measure by which its greatness is recognized and acknowledged. The final measure of the greatness of all peoples is the amount and standard of the literature and art they have produced. The world does not know that a people is great until that people produces great literature and art. No people that has produced great literature and art has ever been looked upon by the world as distinctly inferior. And nothing will do more to ... raise his status than a demonstration of intellectual parity by the Negro through the production of literature and art.[24]

Johnson goes on to talk about black contributions to music, such as spirituals, the widely popular ragtime music, and dance crazes such as the Cakewalk, Turkey Trot, the Eagle Rock, and Ballin' the Jack. He also talks about the nineteenth-century black folktales and the black writers and poets of later years. Johnson's theme, that black music, dance, and literature would undermine racism, was one of the guiding forces behind the Harlem Renaissance.

Langston Hughes and the Weary Blues

Although he promoted black literature, Johnson believed that African American authors should avoid writing in black dialect, which was seen as the speech of the uneducated in inferior classes. This dialect came in two forms. The first was the stereotypical speech of poor southern blacks who said "gwine" instead of "going," "ma" instead of "my," and "mo" for "more." The other black dialect, called Harlemese, was more controversial, and judged like some of the notorious rap music is today. Johnson called Harlemese, or jive, "the common, racy, living authentic speech of the Negro in ... real life."[25] It was the language of jazz musicians or hep cats who called New York City "the Apple," with the main stem of the Apple being Harlem. To use one's brain or apply oneself diligently to a task was called "busting your conk," and someone who was dressed up from head to foot was "togged to the bricks."

While Johnson, along with Du Bois, thought black dialects degraded African Americans in the eyes of whites, many of Harlem's literati thought otherwise. Hughes, who has been called a jazz poet because of the rhythmic, moving character of his words, made a name for himself writing in dialect. Hughes's first major poem "The Weary Blues" won first

Poet Langston Hughes has been called a jazz poet because of the rhythmic, moving character of his words.

prize in the poetry competition held by the literary magazine *Opportunity: A Journal of Negro Life* in 1925. The poem, excerpted below, describes a man listening to an old blues musician in Harlem:

> Droning a drowsy syncopated tune,
> Rocking back and forth to a mellow croon,
> I heard a Negro play.
> Down on Lenox Avenue the other night....
> With his ebony hands on each ivory key
> He made that poor piano moan with melody....
> I heard that Negro sing, that old piano moan—
> "Ain't got nobody in all this world,
> Ain't got nobody but ma self.
> I's gwine to quit ma frownin'
> And put ma troubles on the shelf."[26]

Reviewers loved "The Weary Blues," which appeared with other poems in a 1926 book of the same title. But when Hughes published his second book of poems, *Fine Clothes to the Jew*, the next year, he was roundly criticized. The title, which upset Jewish people, refers to a man who was so poor he had to pawn his suit to a Jewish pawnbroker for a few nickels. The main criticism, however, came from the black press because of the way Hughes portrayed the reality of black urban life. As Hughes describes it in his 1940 autobiography, *The Big Sea*, black critics called the book "a disgrace to the race, a return to the dialect tradition, and a parading of all our racial defects before the public....

In anything white people were likely to read, [black intellectuals] wanted to put their best foot forward, their politely polished and cultural foot—and only that foot.... [When] Negroes wrote books they wanted them to be books in which only good Negroes, clean and cultured and not-funny Negroes, beautiful and nice and upper class were presented."[27]

Reaction was fierce. The Pittsburgh Courier ran a big headline, "LANGSTON HUGHES' BOOK OF POEMS TRASH." The headline in the New York *Amsterdam News* was "LANGSTON HUGHES—THE SEWER DWELLER." The Chicago *Whip* made a play on the words *poet laureate*, a title of respect, and called Hughes "the poet low-rate of Harlem."[28]

A New Day

In his defense, Hughes argued that while he sympathized with the critics' point of view, he simply did not know anybody who was "wholly beautiful and wholly good."[29] And being of modest means himself, he did not even know what life was like for upper-class blacks who went to the elite Harvard University and listened to classical music. So he wrote about his life, his world, and the people who populated it, ignoring the criticism. But Hughes was gaining fame during a period that was particularly sensitive for black authors. For the first time, the powerful New York publishing world was paying close attention, and there was much soul-searching among authors as to how they portrayed African Americans.

In 1923 a mainstream, national publishing company printed Jean Toomer's *Cane*, an experimental novel that mixes poetry and narrative prose about African American life in the rural South and urban North. *Cane* not only describes injustice and prejudice with angry prose, but also describes the compelling beauty of black culture. Commenting on the quality of Toomer's writing, critic William Stanley Braithwaite wrote, "*Cane* is a book of gold and bronze, of dusk and flame, of ecstasy and pain, and Jean Toomer is a bright morning star of a new day in the Race in literature."[30]

In 1924 another major publishing house released Jessie Fauset's book, *There Is Confusion*, which depicts the lives of middle-class African American families from a woman's perspective. Fauset's characters are based on the world she knew. They had been in the United States for many generations, were somewhat affluent and, like many white families of that era, placed great importance on class, pedigree, and manners. Fauset based her novel on her belief that blacks and whites in the middle class shared more cultural similarities than was widely acknowledged. She said,

> I have depicted something of the home life of the colored American who is not being pressed too hard by the Furies of Prejudices, Ignorance, Economic Injustice…. And behold, he is not so vastly different from any other American.[31]

There Is Confusion was widely praised by both black and white reviewers, although one publisher who had rejected the book scoffed, "White readers just don't expect Negroes to be like this."[32]

Finding a New Soul

Writer and sociologist Charles S. Johnson hoped to address the perception gap between black and white by planning a banquet to celebrate the publication of Fauset's novel. Johnson was editor of *Opportunity: A Journal of Negro Life*, the official publication of the National Urban League (NUL), an organization founded to help advance the economic interests of black Americans.

On March 21, 1924, Johnson hosted the NUL Civic Club Dinner where Harlem stars such as Langston Hughes, poet Countee Cullen, and James Weldon Johnson were honored along with Fauset. Johnson also invited white writers, editors, and critics from New York's powerful literary establishment. This event, attended by more than one hundred people, stimulated great interest in black writers among white publishers and is considered the formal launching of the Negro Literary Renaissance. Looking back on the event in later years, Hughes was prompted to write "Charles Johnson did more to encourage and develop Negro writers during the 1920's than anyone else in America."[33]

Paul U. Kellogg, one of the attendees at the Civic Club Dinner, was editor of the *Survey Graphic*, a popular illustrated magazine that focused on poverty, racism, education, working conditions, political reform, and other sociological issues. Inspired by the burgeoning black

Alain Locke was the first to use the word renaissance *in reference to the literary and art movements growing out of Harlem in the 1920s.*

literary movement, Kellogg decided to devote the entire March 1925 issue of the *Survey Graphic* to the art and literature of Harlem. The "Harlem Issue" was edited by writer, philosopher, and educator Alain Locke and remains one of the most detailed accounts of that era. The issue was such a success that Locke expanded it into a book, *The New Negro*, which explores the writing, art, and literary criticism of the Harlem Renaissance. In the introduction to *The New Negro*, Locke explains the significance of the movement:

> Negro life is not only establishing new contacts and founding new centers, it is also finding a new soul. There is a fresh spiritual and cultural focusing. We have, as a heralding sign, an unusual outburst of creative expression. There is a renewed race-spirit that consciously and proudly sets itself apart. Justifiably then, we speak of the offerings of this book embodying these ripening forces as culled from the first fruits of the Negro Renaissance.[34]

"Fy-ah Gonna Burn Ma Soul!"

Locke was the first to use the word *renaissance* in reference to the movement and *The New Negro* and the *Survey Graphic* introduced white readers for the first time to the works of Cullen, McKay, Toomer, Hughes, and others. One of the most vivacious members of the group, Zora Neale Hurston, was a latecomer to the renaissance, moving to Harlem in 1925. Born around the turn of the twentieth century in Eatonville, an all-black community in Florida, Hurston was known more for her humor, use of old-style slave dialect, and outsized charm than her literary accomplishments. (Most of her critically acclaimed work was written in the 1930s after the formal end of the Harlem Renaissance.)

It was Hurston, along with novelist Wallace Thurman, who coined the irreverent term *Niggerati*, a twist on the term *literati* or literary intellectuals, to describe the writers of the renaissance. She gained notice after contributing several short stories to *Opportunity* while attending Barnard College on a scholarship. After moving to New York, the independent, outspoken woman with a rich, commanding voice quickly became a central figure among the Niggerati.

Stories of Hurston's exploits are legendary. She smoked cigarettes in public, which was considered disgraceful for a woman at the time. On one occasion, she took a nickel from the cup of a blind beggar for bus fare, promising to repay it later. And she lived scandalously in a house full of men, including Thurman and painter Richard Bruce Nugent. Hurston jokingly referred to the house on West 136th Street as "Niggerati Manor" and the place was known for its wild parties as Theophilius Lewis wrote in his "Harlem Sketchbook" column in the *Amsterdam News*:

> The story goes out that the bathtubs in the house [are] always packed

Writer Zora Neale Hurston, along with novelist Wallace Thurman, coined the term Niggerati, *a twist on the term* literati *or literary intellectuals, to describe the writers of the Harlem Renaissance.*

with sourmash [whiskey], while gin [flows] from all the water taps and the flush boxes [behind the toilets are] filled with … beer…. In the case of Niggerati Manor, a great deal more smoke [comes] out of the windows than [is] warranted by the size of the fire in the [furnace].[35]

The allusion to smoke might have inspired Hurston, Thurman, Nugent, and painter Aaron Douglas to collaborate on the magazine *Fire!!* in 1926. Although short-lived, the quarterly was the only publication of the renaissance produced by the artists and writers of the movement.

The group chose the name Fire!!, according to Hughes because the idea was to "burn up a lot of the old, dead conventional Negro-white ideas of the past."[36] It featured articles that mocked and scorned the literary establishment, celebrated jazz and blues music, and discussed forbidden topics such as homosexuality and pagan religious beliefs. The foreword to the magazine was enough to frighten some readers. It said,

> FIRE … flaming, burning, searing, and penetrating
> far beneath the superficial items of the flesh to boil the sluggish blood… .
> FIRE … melted steel and iron bars, poking livid
> tongues between stone apertures and burning
> wooden opposition with a crackling chuckle of
> contempt

> Fy-ha,
> Fy-ah, Lawd,
> Fy-ah gonna burn ma soul![37]

Older black intellectuals such as Du Bois were shocked by the unseemly tone of *Fire!!* and the literary critic for the *Baltimore Afro-American* sneered "I have just tossed the first issue of *Fire* into the fire."[38]

Each issue cost the equivalent of four thousand dollars to produce, and it was nearly impossible to get white magazine dealers to distribute the magazine. While teetering on the edge of collapse, the magazine met an ironic end. Most of the copies of *Fire!!* were destroyed when a fire swept through the basement of an apartment where they were stored.

The ill-fated project had a mixed effect on the Harlem literati. On one hand it strengthened the bonds of community between the writers who now understood there was indeed a Negro Literary Renaissance taking place. On the other hand, the demise of the quarterly left black writers beholden to established white publishers who controlled what was acceptable and was not.

While standing in the ashes of *Fire!!*, Hurston's Niggarati could not see into the future. However, many who survived that era went on to respectable careers as authors, poets, and educators. Hardened in the fires of prejudice, segregation, and disappointment, they provided a unique perspective on black life in the United States for many decades to come.

Chapter Three

The Jazz Age

The Harlem Renaissance can be divided into two separate movements, the high and the low. The art and literature of the era was created by those who wanted to prove to white society that African Americans were capable of making "high art" that would appeal to intellectuals and be a positive contribution to American culture. This was seen by some as a way in which black people could secure economic and social equality. As Charles S. Johnson, one of the leaders of the Harlem literary scene put it, African Americans could use the arts to make "a crack in the wall of racism."[39]

"Low art," as it was called by intellectuals, revolved around what was widely known as the devil's music—loud and raucous jazz and blues that emanated from speakeasies, dance halls, and after-hours clubs. Fueled by bootleg liquor, marijuana, and cocaine, the music was wild and erotic and incredibly popular with both black and white audiences. Consequently, the music made a much bigger cultural impact than the Negro Literary Renaissance.

There was great division between the literati and the musicians. The writers often felt the "low art" of the jazz and blues players enforced negative stereotypes about African Americans. Critics felt the music was a perpetuation of racist minstrel shows from the nineteenth century, where black or white entertainers would perform in blackface makeup and mock African Americans for being lazy, superstitious, and only good for playing music or dancing. For their part, the musicians were amused by intellectuals they referred to as "dicty," Harlemese for smart. Composer Fletcher Henderson even immortalized the literati in the song "Dicty's Blues," while Duke Ellington wrote the song "Dicty Glide."

Jazz and Bathtub Gin

Whatever the Harlem literati thought of the music, the era of the Harlem Renaissance is also known as the Jazz Age. The word *Jazz* was originally a black slang term for making love, but it became part of the American lexicon during the Roaring Twenties. Fashionable clothes were called "jazz dresses," modern syncopated verse was called "jazz poetry," and customized old cars were called "jazzy jalopies." But first and foremost, jazz identified the swinging music that was heard everywhere in Harlem, floating out of radios and record players in barber shops and beauty parlors and played by live bands at dance halls, cabarets, and clubs. And it attracted white partiers to Harlem as never before, including the most rich and famous celebrities of the day.

It was not just the music that brought whites to Harlem. In January 1919, the Eighteenth Amendment was added to the Constitution, prohibiting the manufacture, sale, or transportation of

A crowd responds enthusiastically as Cootie Williams plays trumpet with Duke Ellington's band at the Savoy Ballroom in Harlem. The raucous music of the time period was considered "low art" by black intellectuals, but was enormously influential.

intoxicating liquors. The law, known as Prohibition, profoundly influenced American life. While drugs such as marijuana, opium, heroin, and cocaine were legal at that time, it was impossible to lawfully purchase a beer or a shot of whiskey. This prompted millions of Americans to break the law. Many began making their own booze at home, mixing industrial-grade grain alcohol with juniper flavorings used to make gin. The tall bottles that stored this so-called rotgut were topped off with water from the bathtub faucet to produce the final product, bathtub gin.

Those who wanted a real drink were forced to work with gangsters who imported, or bootlegged, whiskey and beer from Canada and elsewhere. It was sold in illicit clubs called speakeasies, most of

Harlem's Musical Scene

The Harlem Renaissance encompassed literature, art, and serious theater, but it was the music that was most widely embraced by white Americans. In his book Harlem Speaks, *Harlem Renaissance scholar Cary D. Wintz discusses the music of the era:*

African American music differed from literature and art in several significant ways. First, African Americans had already proven their creativity in music long before the onset of the literary Renaissance. Rising out of minstrel shows, vaudeville, and the so-called "Coon shows" of the late nineteenth century, songwriting and performing acts … dominated the popular music industry … in the early years of the twentieth century. At the same time, the new sound of jazz emerged from the black sections of New Orleans, and W.C. Handy gave birth to the blues in Memphis. Unlike literature, black musical innovations like jazz and the blues developed in other parts of the country and then exported to New York.

In the years prior to World War I the new musical sounds came to New York and to Harlem. Ragtime first hit the black clubs … [when] ragtime creator Scott Joplin relocated to New York in 1907. W.C. Handy followed in 1918. By that time James Reese Europe's band had assumed the title of the first jazz band in New York City…. By this time Harlem's musical scene was in full swing. Blues singers accompanied jazz bands or sang as headliners and in the early 1920s began recording and selling phonograph records. By the end of the decade the Duke Ellington Orchestra and other musical acts were broadcast nightly from coast to coast.

Cary D. Wintz, ed., *Harlem Speaks: A Living History of the Harlem Renaissance.* Naperville, IL: Sourcebooks, 2007, pp. 148–149.

which were run by organized crime syndicates.

With the price of an illicit drink soaring from twenty-five cents in 1920 to two dollars in 1925, hundreds of illegal drinking establishments opened in Harlem where there were several on every commercial block. The illegal booze attracted adventurous young white people who spent freely and danced to black jazz musicians playing suggestive new dances, such as the Black Bottom and the Charleston.

A Clash of Cultures

With this influx of moneyed customers, Harlem was booming with speakeasies, cellars, lounges, cafes, taverns, supper clubs, rib joints, and numerous bars and grills. With over 125 entertainment places serving both black and white clientele, the African American character of

The Cotton Club in Harlem was the most famous nightclub in the United States. The white-owned club, however, denied black people entry unless they were entertaining the all-white crowds.

Harlem quickly changed. And the white customers were not average Americans. Many were said to be afflicted by "Harlemania," a nearly hysterical love of the neighborhood, and some were members of international high society. Among those visiting Harlem in their Stutz, Packard, or Daimler touring cars were Gertrude Vanderbilt Whitney, granddaughter of railroad magnate Cornelius Vanderbilt; French princess Violette Murat; German-born financier Otto Kahn; movie star Harold Lloyd; and Lady Patricia Mountbatten, wife of British navel commander Lord Mountbatten. These people were observed in expensive restaurants, or at "low-down" speakeasies when they wanted to go "slumming."

Of course there was a negative side to all this attention from high society. African American customers were barred from several of the best restaurants, where only the staff and entertainers were black. A typical example was the gangster-owned Cotton Club, which was the most famous nightclub in the United States. Located on Lenox Avenue, the Cotton Club denied black people entry unless they were entertaining the all-white crowds. The majority of African Americans resented the white incursion into their neighborhood and the exclusionary policies, known as Jim Crow laws. According to Langston Hughes,

> Harlem Negroes did not like the Cotton Club and never appreciated its Jim Crow policy in the very heart of the dark community. Nor

did ordinary Negroes like the growing influx of whites towards Harlem after sundown, flooding the little cabarets and bars where formerly only colored people laughed and sang, and where now strangers were given the best ringside tables to sit and stare at the Negro customers—like amusing animals in a zoo.[40]

However, as Hughes also pointed out, many of the clubs that banned African Americans were not successful. He said, "They failed to realize that a large part of the Harlem attraction was watching the colored customers amuse themselves."[41]

The Stride Piano

Whatever the motivation of the Harlem audiences, there is little doubt that the renaissance offered steady employment to talented black musicians and singers. There were at least fifteen major jazz bands and one hundred lesser-known ensembles that played in the neighborhood throughout the Roaring Twenties. These musicians were from all over the United States, and they influenced what came to be known as the Harlem jazz sound.

The roots of jazz can be traced to late-nineteenth-century New Orleans, where African American musicians blended several forms of traditional music, including work songs, field hollers, blues, ragtime, Mardi Gras marches, and European military music to create a completely new sound. Ragtime was

Scott Joplin was the king of ragtime, a very influential style of music in Harlem.

particularly influential in Harlem. This style is defined by pianists who play complicated songs where the player's right hand "tickles" the keys with a strong rhythmic melody while the left hand plays an intricate bass part.

Scott Joplin was the king of ragtime, and his 1899 composition "Maple Leaf Rag," was the first instrumental to sell over 1 million copies of sheet music. Joplin moved to Harlem in 1907, and his music evolved into the "stride piano" style adopted by New York musicians. Stride pianists play percussive, "striding" chords with one hand while tickling the melody on the upper keys with the other. The sound is so large and powerful, that it could be described as orchestral, or sounding like a full orchestra.

The keyboardists called themselves "ticklers" but gave each other rowdy nicknames, such as "the Bear," "the Beetle," "the Beast," and "the Brute," which accurately portrayed their prowess on the piano. Harlem's most famous ticklers were Willie "the Lion" Smith,

The Everlovin' Stomp

Most residents of Harlem were unable to afford the expensive clubs patronized by whites and the Talented Tenth. In fact some were so poor that they had to throw "rent parties," where attendees would crowd into an apartment and contribute ten to fifty cents toward the host's rent. The parties lasted until dawn and the entertainment could be spectacular. One of Harlem's leading piano ticklers, Willie "the Lion" Smith describes rent parties from a musician's perspective:

Piano players called these affairs jumps or shouts…. It got so we never stopped and we were up and down Fifth, Seventh, and Lenox all night long hitting the keys…. On a single Saturday [we would] book as many as three parties….

There were, of course, some of the chitterling struts [parties] where a bunch of pianists would be in competition. [Our booking agent] Lippy was a great promoter and was always trying to steam up the guests to argue who was the best. It sometimes got annoying, especially when you had your eyes on a good-looking chick, or wanted to take time out to get in on the [gambling] games they always had going in the back bedrooms. But you had to stay by the keyboard to hold your own reputation for being a fast pianist…. During [the] early hours close to dawn the … lights would be dimmed down and the people would call out to the piano player. "Play it, oh, play it," or "Break it down," or "Get in the gully and give us the everlovin' stomp." Those were happy days.

Quoted in Jervis Anderson, *This Was Harlem*. New York: Farrar Straus Giroux, 1982, pp. 155–156.

Ferdinand "Jelly Roll" Morton, and Fats Waller. But New Jersey–born pianist James P. Johnson perfected the style in Harlem and earned title "the father of stride piano." As jazz musician and historian Mark C. Gridley explains in *Jazz Styles: History and Analysis*, Johnson "perfected the orchestral approach to jazz piano playing, as though he were a one-man band."[42]

In addition to his influential playing style, Johnson was a popular—and prolific—composer who wrote 230 songs, 19 symphonic works, and 11 musicals. But his most famous composition was "The Charleston," which had an accompanying dance. This song brought jazz to a wide audience and became synonymous with the Jazz Age.

The Jungle Sound

Johnson often participated in what were called cutting contests with other notable stride players such as Willie "the Lion" Smith and others. These events, in which pianists attempted to cut each other down, or out play each other with nearly impossible riffs and runs, attracted many young musicians. Among them was up-and-coming pianist Edward "Duke" Ellington, who was awed by Johnson's creative licks, fast hands, and precision runs.

Ellington was born in Washington, D.C., in 1899 and moved to Harlem in 1923. Within a few years, he formed a red-hot band called the Washingtonians. Trumpet player Bubber Miley gave the Washingtonians a unique voice, wringing a down-and-dirty, blues-drenched, "gut bucket" sound from his horn. Ellington called it the "Jungle Sound," and it became synonymous with Harlem jazz.

By 1927 Ellington was pioneering a new type of jazz, composing music that mixed jazz with the lush orchestral sounds heard in popular theatrical musicals. By adding strings, brass, and woodwinds, Ellington forged a distinctive sound all his own. Because Ellington's grand sound appealed to an upper-class white audience, critics called it "sophisticated music."

Ellington's sophisticated new sound developed around the time that his group was hired as the house band for the Cotton Club. The fashionable club was decorated in the style of a nineteenth-century southern mansion. Although it catered only to white people, all the dancers, singers, comedians, and other entertainers were black. The club's music, plantation theme, and raucous dance pieces provided wealthy whites a chance to experience what was called a primitive African or jungle atmosphere.

The ten-piece band, now renamed Duke Ellington and His Cotton Club Orchestra, quickly achieved national fame when its performances were featured on CBS radio broadcasts made from the club every Saturday night. With his newfound fame and money, Ellington was able to hire the best musicians in New York—and write stunning arrangements that allowed them to showcase their talents.

Ellington played Harlem's Cotton Club off and on until 1933. And between

Duke Ellington and his band gained fame by playing their new type of jazz music at the Cotton Club and, later, on national radio and in the movies.

1927 and 1931 his orchestra made 150 records in sixty-four different recording sessions. When not playing and recording in New York, Ellington toured extensively in the United States and Europe. Wherever he played, his manager, Irving Mills, sent out press releases that read: "Come on! Get hot! Get happy! [With] Harlem's jazz king, blaring, crooning, burning up the stage with his red hot rhythms, moaning saxophones, wailing cornets, laughing trombones, screaming clarinets."[43] During his West Coast tours, Ellington brought the Harlem sound to Hollywood movies beginning in 1929 with *Black and Tan Fantasy*, a film named after one of his famous songs.

Ellington's many memorable compositions, such as "Mood Indigo," "It Don't Mean a Thing If It Ain't Got That Swing," and "Sophisticated Lady," utilized catchy and unusual melodies. And although his strutting, swinging sounds became jazz classics across the globe, Ellington's music was firmly rooted in Harlem. In *Black Music in the Harlem Renaissance* music professor Mark Tucker writes:

> Even when touring took him away from home … Ellington continued to celebrate Harlem in music. His compositions described its echoes and air shafts, boys and blue belles [beautiful women]. His songs advised people to drop off there and to slap their soles on Seventh Avenue. His signature piece ("Take the A Train") even told them which train to take [to reach Harlem]. And he paid tribute to his adopted

community in "Beige" … and in "A Tone Parallel to Harlem" … a joyous evocation of Harlem's sounds, street-life, and citizens.[44]

Jungle Alley

While Ellington's music crossed racial and cultural lines, the price of a night at the Cotton Club was equal to a week's wages for the average New York resident. But even those who were not rich—or white—could find a wealth of entertainment in the district known as "Jungle Alley" on 133rd Street between Lenox and Seventh. In *Harlem Speaks* history professor Cary D. Wintz describes the district this way:

> [Jungle Alley] provided a variety of entertainment options and a more eclectic and risqué environment. It catered to a racially mixed and sexually uninhibited clientele. In Jungle Alley everyone rubbed shoulders— gay and straight, whites from across the city, working-class blacks as well as intellectuals, writers, musicians, artists, businessmen, criminals, and prostitutes. They drank bootleg liquor, had access to marijuana and harder drugs, and danced or just listened to jazz and blues artists, often until daybreak.[45]

The "torrid warbler" Gladys Bentley, was a typical entertainer in the district. Working at the Clam House, the 250-pound (113kg) vocalist sang bawdy songs while wearing a man's top hat and tails. She sat at her piano from 10 o'clock in the evening until dawn, playing blues classics such as "The St. James Infirmary" without stopping between songs. According to Hughes,

[She plays] with a powerful and continuous underbeat of jungle rhythm. Miss Bentley was an amazing exhibition of musical energy—a large, dark, masculine lady, whose feet pounded the floor while her fingers pounded the keyboard—a perfect piece of African sculpture, animated by her own rhythm.[46]

The Empress of the Blues

Bentley eventually became so popular she moved to bigger Harlem clubs, then to Hollywood. But she was only one of the Harlem blues royalty to achieve international fame. Bessie Smith, known as "The Empress of the Blues," was among the biggest stars of the Harlem Renaissance.

Smith was born into dire poverty around 1894 in Chattanooga, Tennessee. She was an orphan by the age of nine and was forced to earn a meager living dancing and singing on Chattanooga street corners accompanied by her brother on guitar. At age seventeen Smith was hired as a professional dancer in a black touring show whose star was the legendary singer Gertrude "Ma" Rainey, known as the "Mother of the Blues".

During an era when black women were treated with even less respect than black men, Rainey carried herself as a proud diva. She sang about her life—bad times, cheating men, and crippling loneliness—but demanded respect from her audiences. Smith gained the admiration of Ma Rainey, and the two became inseparable, performing and writing songs together. By the early 1920s, both were major stars, playing on the same bill in theaters packed with integrated audiences.

In the early 1920s, most record companies refused to record black artists. However, after blues singer Mamie Smith (no relation to Bessie) had a few unexpected hits, record companies realized there was a huge demand for what they called "race records." Bessie Smith recorded "Down Hearted Blues," in 1923, and the record sold an astounding 780,000 copies in six months. The money saved Columbia Records, which was nearly bankrupt, but Smith was only paid 250 dollars. (Popular white artists like Al Jolson were paid a royalty for each record sold and quickly became millionaires.) Although her subsequent "race records" sold millions, Smith primarily made her fortune as a performer, earning up to two thousand dollars a week playing various theaters in New York, Chicago, and elsewhere. Describing her talents in their book *Black Magic*, Langston Hughes and Milton Meltzer write, "Bessie did not attempt to entertain. She simply stood still and shouted the blues without trick arrangements or orchestral refinements—and she rocked the joint. Before the days of microphones, Bessie could be heard for a mile."[47]

Blues singer Bessie Smith was one of the biggest musical stars of the Harlem Renaissance.

Bessie Smith was revered by many in Harlem. However, she was promiscuous, and a heavy-drinking brawler who would fight anyone who slighted her. As a result, she was shunned by the Harlem literati, who equated culture with European classical music and opera. According to jazz critic Chip Deffa, upper-class blacks considered Smith "too much of the streets, a rough-edged reminder of lower-class roots they wanted to forget…. Smith was a crude, primitive 'blues shouter' to be ignored."[48] Smith understood the dicty attitudes and offered her feelings about the intellectuals in the 1933 song "Gimme a Pigfoot (and a Bottle of Beer)." In the lyrics of the song, Smith castigates the highbrows for being tightly wound and for dismissing the blues with a tut-tut. In defiance of these attitudes, Smith calls for a hot-stomping piano player and a party until dawn with soul food, beer, gin, and marijuana.

By this time, Smith's career was suffering. Her biggest fans were poor people who could not afford to buy her records after the Great Depression hit in 1929. But "Gimme a Pigfoot" was recorded in a session with jazz greats Jack Teagarden, Benny Goodman, and

Home of Happy Feet

There is a reason the Savoy Ballroom was known as Home of Happy Feet during the Harlem Renaissance. In their book Black Magic, *Langston Hughes and Milton Meltzer explain:*

In the Twenties it seemed as if all Harlem was dancing—and Harlemites set the rest of the world to dancing, too. The leg-flinging Charleston … originated with the kids of Harlem [and] swept the world…. In quick succession for a decade new Negro dances followed, and some caught on with a wide public—the droll Black Bottom, the shim-sham-shimmy with its freeze-in-place break, the pixie-like truckin' raising a pointed finger, and above all the long popular Lindy hop originating at the Savoy Ballroom in 1927…. The Savoy in Harlem, an institution for many years, was a dance emporium known as the Home of Happy Feet, where downtown whites and uptown Negroes came to "trip the light fantastic," clap hands to the Charleston, to truck around the floor with arms akimbo, and to swing out in the Lindy hop, the dance that started the ballroom custom of couples not remaining close together as they as they dance. It was the Lindy that later turned into the rocking rhythms of the jitterbug.

Langston Hughes and Milton Meltzer, *Black Magic*. Englewood Cliffs, NJ: Prentice Hall, 1967, pp. 91–92.

Chu Berry. With this band, Smith was moving beyond the blues and taking jazz in a new direction. But while she was still playing at Harlem clubs like Connie's Inn and the newly opened Apollo Theater, she was only making a small percentage of what she had in the 1920s.

Stompin' at the Savoy

With her low-down blues, Smith had difficulty competing with the lively jazz music that attracted massive crowds to the Savoy, Harlem's hottest nightspot. Covering an entire city block on Lenox Avenue, the Savoy opened in March 1926. Built by a white music promoter and a black businessman for the then-astounding sum of two hundred thousand dollars, the Savoy was an architectural wonder. It featured a huge lobby and a block-long dance hall atop two dazzling mirror-lined, marble staircases.

The dance palace was described as a community ballroom where black or white, rich or poor, local or tourist, could

The Savoy Ballroom was one of the most popular places to dance in Harlem for both white and black patrons.

gain admission for only fifty cents on most nights and seventy-five cents on Sundays. In addition to drawing Harlem's blue-collar crowd of busboys, truck drivers, and domestic servants, the Savoy attracted royalty and stars of the silver screen, including the Prince of Wales, Marlene Dietrich, Greta Garbo, and Lana Turner. On weekends up to four thousand guests packed into the club to hear two bands "stompin' at the Savoy."[49]

Fletcher Henderson and his Rainbow Orchestra was one of the world-class acts that played the Savoy. Another star was drummer Chick Webb, leader of the Chick Webb Orchestra. Webb's driving beat was compared to a railroad train running at full throttle. One of the major features at the Savoy was the Battle of the Bands, where guest bands from New York, Chicago, and New Orleans were pitted against Webb's band. Even jazz greats like Louis Armstrong, Cab Calloway, King Oliver, and Fess Williams feared battling Webb, who was usually judged the winner by the cheering crowd.

Some of the best entertainment at the Savoy was provided free by the dancers who strutted and jumped on the famous 50 by 250 foot (15 by 76m) burnished maple and mahogany dance floor. The floor was a wonder in itself and saw so much shoe leather that it had to be replaced every three years. Many of the dance fads that swept across the United States in the 1920s, such as the Lindy Hop, the Suzy Q, and the Shim-Sham-Shimmy, were invented at the Savoy, which billed itself as "The Home of Happy Feet."

On Tuesday nights, the club hosted the 400 Club which featured professional dancers such as George "Shorty" Snowden, who is often credited with naming the Lindy Hop. The popular dance features pinwheel spins, and "breakaways" in which the female dance partner is thrown and twirled high in the air with wild abandon. Swing dancers still perform the Lindy Hop. On Thursday nights ladies were admitted free to the Savoy for "Kitchen Mechanics' Night," a slang term applied to cooks and maids. Saturday night, however, was known among locals as "Square Night" because it was a time when the fumble-footed "unhip" white downtowners showed up to crowd onto the dance floor.

Although most blacks resented the white patrons at the Savoy and elsewhere, there was a positive aspect to Harlemania. When black and white people got to know one another, social and racial barriers began to fall away. This helped make it fashionable among whites to support "higher" aspects of African American culture, including art, literature, and theater. With this patronage, driven by the sounds of jazz music, the Harlem Renaissance was able to reach a wider audience and make its mark on the Roaring Twenties.

Chapter Four

The Renaissance in Black Theater

Langston Hughes wrote that the Harlem Renaissance began on May 23, 1921, when the musical revue *Shuffle Along* opened at the Sixty-third Street Music Hall above Times Square near Broadway. According to Hughes, *Shuffle Along* "gave a scintillating send-off to that Negro vogue in Manhattan."[50] Many historians question Hughes's assessment, but white people did flock to *Shuffle Along* in droves. And police were forced to convert Sixty-third Street into a one-way thoroughfare to ease the traffic nightmare.

Shuffle Along, according to Hughes, was "a honey of a show, swift bright rollicking, and gay, with a dozen danceable, singable tunes."[51] Written by Flournoy Miller and Aubrey Lyles, with lyrics by Noble Sissle and music by Eubie Blake, the revue was filled with comedy, ragtime music, and jazz dancing. And it was the first major production in many years to be produced, written, and performed entirely by African Americans.

The Lafayette Players

Shuffle Along ran for 504 performances. But eleven years before its "scintillating send-off," black producers, directors, and actors were forming their own theater companies in Harlem. As far back as 1910, black playwrights wrote dramas, comedies, and musicals for upper-class black audiences. These African American theater patrons could afford tickets on Broadway but were either forced to sit in segregated sections in the balconies or banned from the theaters all together.

With African American actors, dancers, and singers also largely banned on Broadway, Harlem productions attracted the most talented black performers in the United States. And they were able to perform plays that reflected on the pain and beauty in their lives. As David Krasner

Actor Clarence Muse mocked the practice of white actors appearing on stage in blackface makeup by appearing in a production of Within the Law *in whiteface.*

writes in his book *A Beautiful Pageant,* "Black theatre explored community issues away from white audiences and the demand to please them."[52]

By 1914 there were several theaters in Harlem with their own repertory stock companies, that is, permanent groups of actors, directors, and stage technicians. The most famous, the Lafayette Theater Company, was founded by Lester Walton, amusement critic for *New York Age,* and Anita Bush, known as "the Little Mother of Negro Drama." The Lafayette Players presented a variety of entertainment, including musicals, comedies, grand operas, and the plays of Shakespeare. Their most popular productions, however, were uptown Harlem performances of downtown Broadway hits. These plays with all-black casts included *Dr. Jekyll and Mr. Hyde, The Count of Monte Cristo,* and even the Jewish comedy *Potash and Perlmutter.* However, the play *Within the Law* attracted widespread attention after lawyer-turned-actor Clarence Muse mocked the common practice of white actors appearing in blackface makeup. Hughes and Meltzer explain:

Ebony-dark Clarence Muse made a great hit—performing the role of the lawyer in whiteface. Muse, who had enormous popularity with Harlem audiences and whose rich deep voice was well known, used a gimmick in [*Within the Law*] which never failed to bring the house down. At his initial entrance, Muse first began to speak off stage, carrying on a brief conversation while still out of sight. The audience would think, "There comes Clarence," but they were unprepared for what was to happen—the very dark Muse stepped on stage *completely white.* Astonished pandemonium always broke out. Applause shook the theatre. *Within the Law* in Harlem became an S.R.O. [standing room only] hit.[53]

Muse later became a writer, director, and producer as well as one of the most famous black actors in Hollywood during the 1940s. But Muse was just one among many fine actors in the company that included Abbie Mitchell, Laura Bowman, Charles Gilpin, Hilda Simms, and Frank Wilson. These actors exuded so much talent that they began attracting white crowds from downtown. As Walton wrote in 1920:

It is beginning to dawn on the managers and actor folk on Broadway that something worthy of more than passing consideration to those interested in the drama is taking place weekly at the Lafayette Theatre further uptown. No longer are the Lafayette Players ... referred to in a jocular manner.... Nowadays stage celebrities in goodly numbers are wending their way to Seventh Avenue and 131st St. by limousine to look upon the efforts of these colored thespians with serious eye.[54]

Serious Attention

The Lafayette Players honed their skills in Harlem. But in April 1917 many of them participated in another groundbreaking event when they appeared in *Three Plays for the Negro Theatre* at the Garden Theater on Broadway. The three one-act plays, written by white playwright Ridgely Torrence and produced with two white collaborators, featured an all-black cast of actors. James Weldon Johnson recalls the significance of this event in his 1930 book, *Black Manhattan*, writing that the opening of *Three Plays for the Negro Theatre* is "the most important single event in the entire history of the Negro in the American theatre…. It was the first time anywhere in the United States the Negro actors in the dramatic theatre commanded the serious attention of the critics and of the *general* press and public."[55]

Three Plays for the Negro Theatre did not run for long—the day after it opened the United States entered World War I. However, the production was a milestone because it was the first time that black artists appeared in serious roles on Broadway and showed complex human emotions and yearnings. And it was viewed within the African American community as a resounding rejection of

Emperor Jones

When all-black casts began appearing in Broadway plays in the early 1920s, it was viewed as a major accomplishment for African Americans. However, judged by today's standards, the plays might be seen as racially insensitive, if not blatantly offensive. For example, in Shuffle Along *several of the characters are swindlers, who only view light-skinned black women as desirable. Even a serious play such as* The Emperor Jones *perpetuated the stereotypical image of the uncivilized, uneducated Southern black man. In the play, character Brutus Jones describes his life of crime:*

Maybe I goes to jail dere for gettin' in an argument wid razors ovah a crap game. Maybe I gits twenty years when dat colored man die. Maybe I gits in 'nother argument wid de prison guard was overseer ovah us when we're wukin' de roads. Maybe he hits me wid a whip and I splits his head wid a shovel and runs away and files de chain off my leg and gits away safe. Maybe I does all dat an' maybe I don't. It's a story I tells you so's you knows I'se de kind of man dat if you evah repeats one words of it, I ends yo' stealin' on dis yearth mighty damn quick!

Eugene O'Neill, *The Emperor Jones*, www.eoneill.com/texts/jones/i.htm.

the trivial humor and stereotypes perpetuated by traditional minstrel shows.

The Emperor Jones

It took three years for another drama with an African American cast to appear on Broadway. *The Emperor Jones*, written by white author Eugene O'Neill, is the story of Brutus Jones, a convicted black murderer who escapes from prison to an unnamed island in the Caribbean where he uses his skills as a con artist to become emperor.

The Emperor Jones starred Charles Gilpin in the first important role written for a black actor. However, Jones speaks

Actor Charles Gilpin portraying Brutus Jones in The Emperor Jones. *This was the first important role written expressly for a black actor.*

a crude black Southern dialect, and his character perpetuates the stereotypical view of the African American male as a swindler, huckster, and dangerous criminal. Commenting on this aspect of the play, the *Boston Globe* praised Gilpin, writing that "only an actor of genuine power could save some of [the scenes] from becoming ludicrous."[56] For his part, Gilpin often changed the dialogue—much to O'Neill's displeasure—using terms such as *black baby, Negro,* or *colored man* in place of offensive racial slurs.

Whatever the criticism, *The Emperor Jones* was an overnight success after its November 1, 1920, premier in the Provincetown Theatre off Broadway. After causing lines around the block and thousands of demands for tickets, the production was moved to a larger theater on Broadway and extra shows were added. For his role in the play, Gilpin was awarded the NAACP Spingarn Medal for the highest achievement of an American Negro.

While racial stereotypes were largely overlooked in *The Emperor Jones,* O'Neill's next play, *All God's Chillun Got Wings,* was seen as offensive to whites. Starring black actor Paul Robeson and white actress Mary Blair, *All God's Chillun* was about interracial marriage and called for Robeson to kiss Blair's hand onstage. When the press was notified of this provocative storyline, many newspaper editorial boards demanded that the play be banned. This inflamed the public and the cast was deluged with death threats. Although there was fear that riots would break out or the theater would be bombed, the debate only fueled demand for tickets. *All God's Chillun* opened peacefully in November 1924 and the hullabaloo helped catapult Robeson and Blair to international stardom.

"Watchin' New Miracles Every Day"

By the time *All God's Chillun* premiered, *Shuffle Along* was being performed by road companies in packed theaters across the United States. The play "legitimized the black musical, [spawned] dozens of imitators, [and made African American musicals] a Broadway staple,"[57] according to theater historian Allen Woll. Some of those imitators included *Put and Take, Strut Miss Lizzie, Plantation Revue, Runnin' Wild,* and *Lucky Sambo.*

Despite the historic role of *Shuffle Along,* the play was almost doomed before it started. No black musical comedy had opened on Broadway since 1910, and those that premiered in earlier times were not successful. And, as Lester A. Walton, editor of *New York Age,* explained in 1924, white promoters would not produce black revues because, "white amusement seekers would not patronize a colored show as a legitimate theatrical proposition. Negro entertainment [was regarded] merely as a lure for slumming parties [only suitable on] the fringe of the theatre district."[58]

The creators of *Shuffle Along* overcame these difficulties through sheer talent. Flournoy Miller and Aubrey Lyles were known for their hilarious comedy routines on the vaudeville circuit. (Vaudeville

Noble Sissle and Eubie Blake wrote most of the music for the black musical Shuffle Along.

was a type of popular entertainment that featured singing, dancing, and comedy acts.) Noble Sissle and Eubie Blake, known as the Dixie Duo, were also established vaudeville stars. Blake, the most famous of the crew, began playing the organ when he was five years old, composed "Charleston Rag" on the piano when he was twelve, and was playing keyboards with Big Jim Europe's jazz band when he was eighteen. He had written most of the music for *Shuffle Along* with Sissle long before the play premiered. However, the Dixie Duo could not get white producers to buy their songs and publish them as sheet music, which was

the road to riches in the early twentieth century.

In 1920 the creators of *Shuffle Along* were struggling to produce a play, conceived primarily for black audiences, on Broadway, the most competitive entertainment environment in the world. With no outside financing, they were forced to pay for rehearsals with their vaudeville salaries. Many of the actors, singers, and dancers worked for free, hoping for a big payday when the show began playing.

Shuffle Along opened first in Washington, D.C., in early 1921. After two successful weeks, and a short run in Philadelphia, the producers were able to take it to New York. Amazed that the show went on despite their shoestring budget, Blake later remarked:

I still don't know how we did it. We didn't have money for *nothin'*—not for train fare when we needed it, not for scenery. It just seemed that we *found* everything just when we needed it. I believe if something is *meant* to happen, it's *going* to happen. That's how we *all* felt! It was like watchin' new miracles every day.[59]

The money shortage also meant that Blake and the others could not hire big-name stars. However, after *Shuffle Along* was successful, several of the singers and dancers found stardom. Josephine Baker became the toast of Broadway and an international sensation nearly overnight after she appeared in the show's chorus line. Florence Mills, a cabaret singer and comic, was soon the top black star in America and went on to perform to critical acclaim in London, Paris, and other European cities. Sheet music and records

"She Shook and Shimmied"

Josephine Baker became an international star nearly overnight after first appearing in the chorus line of *Shuffle Along* at the age of seventeen. But Baker was not hired for her stunning beauty. Instead she impressed the show's musical producer, Eubie Blake, with her comedic dance performances, mugging, crossing her eyes, making faces, tripping, falling out of step with the other dancers, and humorously rushing to catch up. When she appeared before audiences, she quickly stole the show and was soon one of the most popular and well-paid members of the cast. Within months, this light-skinned African American woman who grew up in dire poverty in St. Louis, Missouri, became the first international sex symbol of the twentieth century.

After a triumphant run in *Shuffle Along*, Baker appeared in *Chocolate Dandies*. But Baker could not endure American racism. In 1925 she fled Harlem and embarked on an extremely successful career in Paris. Her dance routines highlighted seemingly impossible contorted dances patterned on the movements of African animals. Author Phyllis Rose describes Baker's dancing: "She splayed her arms and legs as if they were dislocated. She shook and shimmied constantly, moving like a snake.... Finally she left the stage on all fours, legs stiff, rear end in the air, higher than her head, looking as awkward as a young giraffe." When not imitating animals, Baker created near riots parading down Paris streets with a pet leopard on a leash.

Quoted in Cary D. Wintz, ed., *Harlem Speaks: A Living History of the Harlem Renaissance*. Naperville, IL: Sourcebooks, 2007, p. 314.

of songs from the revue also became worldwide hits including "I'm Just Wild About Harry," "Bandana Days," "Love Will Find a Way," and "In Honeysuckle Time."

Blake also became a major star. During intermission on opening night, white audience members were so astounded that they approached him just to touch his hand or coat sleeve. Commenting on this phenomenon, Blake stated, "Well you got to feel that. It made me feel like, well, at last, I'm a human being."[60]

After the success of *Shuffle Along*, Sissle and Blake wrote other popular musicals, including the *Chocolate Dandies* which featured Baker. Blake also did solo projects, such as the musical *Blackbirds* featuring Mills and Ethel Waters and dancer Bojangles. *Blackbirds of 1928* featured songs such as "Diga Diga Doo," and "I Can't Give You Anything But Love," that became international hits. Other popular black revues that played Broadway in the wake of *Shuffle Along* included *Rang Tang, Keep Shufflin'*, and the Fats Waller production *1929 Hot Chocolates*.

The Finest Negro Actors

African American comedy revues were beloved by black and white audiences. However, some of the intellectuals behind the New Negro renaissance were appalled upon seeing African American comedians performing in heavy blackface makeup on Broadway. Alain Locke and James Weldon Johnson wrote "we did not enthuse"[61] seeing African Americans cater to white stereotypes in *Shuffle*

Along. But whatever the criticism of the literati crowd, they were doubtlessly pleased that successful African American revues paved the way for a second wave of dramatic plays with black casts. Some of these shows, written mostly by white playwrights, were credited with accurately depicting black life in the United States.

Black Experience Portrayed in Plays

In 1926 Paul Green's *In Abraham's Bosom* opened at the Provincetown Theatre. The Pulitzer Prize–winning play portrays a black farmer who struggles against society to obtain an education. In the end he kills his white half brother and is hanged by a mob. Green grew up on a cotton farm in North Carolina, and according to newspaper editor Roy Parker Jr., the play is based on "the shame and outrage that he felt for the atrocities … of the chain gang, and of the discrimination that race and poverty visited on common people."[62]

Dubose Heyward was another white author from the Carolinas who had viewed the plight of southern blacks through sympathetic eyes. His 1924 novel, *Porgy*, tells the story of a handicapped street beggar in the fictitious Catfish Row slum of Charleston, South Carolina. The year after it was published, Heyward's wife Dorothy, an Ohio-born playwright, began adapting it for the stage. The play premiered at the Guild Theatre on Broadway on October 1, 1927. According to Hughes and Meltzer, *Porgy* "featured a cast composed of the finest

Sidney Poitier and Dorothy Dandridge starred in the 1959 movie adaptation of the successful stage musical Porgy and Bess.

Negro actors ever assembled in one production up to that time."[63]

Whatever the talents of its cast, *Porgy* was not within reach of most Harlem residents. The tickets were twenty-five dollars each (a week's pay for an average Harlemite), and moreover, the Guild was a segregated theater. So while Harlem's richest citizens were able to afford a ticket to *Porgy*, they were forced to sit in the "colored section" in the balcony. Nevertheless, as historian David Levering Lewis writes in *When Harlem Was in Vogue*, "Everybody in Harlem seemed to know someone in the cast … [and] *Porgy* was Harlem's play."[64] Cast members, such as Rose McClendon, who played Serena; Frank Wilson, who played Porgy; Evelyn Ellis, who played Bess; and Percy Verwayne, who played Sportin' Life, were well-known bohemians who hung around a Harlem club known as the Dark Tower. In addition, the street corners and storefront churches on *Porgy's* Catfish Row were based on director Rouben Mamoulian's tours through Harlem. And since many residents of the neighborhood had read the book, Lewis notes, "Harlemites knew the

The Miracle of Green Pastures

In his book Black Manhattan, *James Weldon Johnson highly praises the cast of* The Green Pastures *and its creator Marc Connelly:*

[I]n previous dramas the] Negro removed any lingering doubts as to his ability to do intelligent acting. In *The Green Pastures* he established conclusively his capacity to get the utmost subtleties across the footlights, to convey the most delicate nuances of emotion, to create the atmosphere in which the seemingly unreal becomes for the audience the most real thing in life. *The Green Pastures* is a play so simple and yet so profound, so close to the earth and yet so spiritual, that it is as high a test for those powers in the actor as any play the American stage has seen—a higher test than many of the immortalized classics…. The acting in *The Green Pastures* seems so spontaneous and natural that one is tempted to believe the players are not really acting. In the light of the truth about the matter, this is a high compliment…. What Mr. Connelly actually did was to work something very little short of a miracle. No one seems able to remember any playwright, play, and company of players that have together received such unanimous praise as these … in the making of *The Green Pastures*.

James Weldon Johnson, *Black Manhattan*. New York: Da Capo, 1991, pp. 218–219.

lines of the play almost as well as the understudies did."[65]

Porgy ran for 850 performances and was considered one of the greatest dramas of the Harlem Renaissance. It was remade in 1935 into the opera *Porgy and Bess* with music by George Gershwin and lyrics by Ira Gershwin and Dorothy Heyward. *Porgy and Bess* was revived again in 1959 by MGM for a film version featuring an all-star African American cast that included Sidney Poitier, Dorothy Dandridge, Sammy Davis Jr., Pearl Bailey, and Diahann Carroll.

Changes in the Air

Before starring in *Porgy*, Frank Wilson was a Harlem mailman who wrote plays in his spare time. After becoming a Broadway star, Wilson used his connections to produce a play he had written called *Meek Mose*. According to Lewis, the play, which opened February 6, 1928, "provided employment for every professional Afro-American actor [in Harlem] and a few relatives besides."[66] Harlem residents were also proud that New York mayor Jimmy Walker addressed the crowd on opening night at the Princess

White writer Marc Connelly wrote the play The Green Pastures *about African American religious beliefs.*

Theater. Moreover, other politicians and members of the city's upper classes were in attendance. However, some were upset by the racial stereotypes in the play, and most critics were not impressed as a 1928 review in *Time* reveals:

Meek Mose, in acting and writing, was irreparably inept. It tells of an aged darky [Negro] and the slap, slap, slap of life as he turned the other cheek. The inevitable chant of spirituals saved the night from utter rout.[67]

Meek Mose closed before February ended and by this time a series of events had begun shaking the foundations of African American theater on Broadway. In November 1927, Florence Mills had died unexpectedly from acute appendicitis at the height of her fame. Meanwhile, Harlem Renaissance promoters Alain Locke, James Weldon Johnson, and W.E.B. Du Bois had moved on to new interests and were paying less attention to black theater and drama. More devastating, a new technology created irresistible competition for Broadway. In 1927 the era of the silent movie ended when the first films with sound, called "talkies," were introduced to the public. Talkies drew audiences, actors, and writers away from live theater and attendance fell dramatically. Then in October 1929, a massive stock market crash signaled the beginning of the Great Depression. Four months later, *The Green Pastures* opened at the Mansfield Theater.

The Green Pastures, written by white author Marc Connelly, focuses on African American tales of spirituality based on Bible stories and biblical figures. Featuring black angels, choirs, and a character called De Lawd (the Lord), Connelly described his work as "an attempt to present certain aspects of a living religion in the terms of its believers. The religion is that of thousands of Negroes in the deep South."[68]

The Green Pastures was universally praised. With songs performed by the Hall Johnson Choir and Richard B. Harrison playing De Lawd, *The Green Pastures* played for 557 sold-out performances. The play was then taken on extensive tours in both the North and South before returning to Broadway for a five-year run.

"We Gave It All We Had"

The Green Pastures was the last great African American drama of the Harlem Renaissance. By the time of its debut, the United States was in the grip of an unprecedented economic disaster. Many of New York's millionaires lost everything, while more than one-third of American adults were unemployed. In this environment, African Americans were the first to be fired and this trend even affected Broadway producers and entertainers. Although *Shuffle Along* had made an astounding 8 million dollars, Eubie Blake found himself working less and filling his idle hours by playing pool all day. When he tried to revive his famous hit as *Shuffle Along 1933*, the revue closed after only two weeks. Commenting on the failure, Blake said, "We saw it wasn't going anywhere.... It wasn't the show, it was the times…. So we went on the road. We really worked. We gave it all we had. But it was no use. We got to L.A. and didn't even have enough money left to get us home."[69]

Blake was lucky. He was able to make ends meet by conducting his dance band and writing musicals subsidized by a federal program called the Works Progress Administration (WPA). As part of President Franklin D. Roosevelt's New Deal program to aid the unemployed, the WPA assisted many artists, writers, and entertainers with government grants. But for the average resident of Harlem, the Depression erased the small gains provided by the renaissance. And the magic of Broadway would do nothing to change that. The stage lights dimmed and the Harlem Renaissance faded to black.

Chapter Five

A Renaissance in Art

In 1907 renowned artist Pablo Picasso visited the Ethnological Museum in Paris, France. The museum was filled with ancient African masks and statues, called fetishes. These sculptures were said to have supernatural powers. They were created by African shamans who used them to communicate with mystical spirits in order to attract luck, heal the sick, and ward off evil.

Picasso was deeply moved by the African art and when he returned to his studio, he incorporated the masks into a shocking new painting, *The Young Ladies of Avignon*. With its abstract and elongated faces and triangular features inspired by the African sculptures, Picasso's painting style was both ancient and shockingly new. Critics called the technique cubism and countless cubist paintings were produced by Picasso and others in the decades that followed. This new genre was extremely popular among collectors and heralded a revival of the declining European art market.

While Europeans marveled at Picasso's melding of traditional and modern art, American critics were less impressed. In 1926 collector Albert C. Barnes commented on the African influence on European art:

To persons who understood either the distinguished aesthetic ancestry of Negro sculpture or the psychological makeup of the Negro himself, it is not … surprising that the failing powers of European art should have been revived by the art of the Negro…. The greatest traditions of antiquity were … the birthright of the Negro…. The place of the Negro in modern art is not that of … an intruder, but of one who belongs there by natural right and artistic inheritance.[70]

"Good, Truth, and Beauty"

Despite Barnes's comments, most African American artists had to imitate European painters and sculptors in order to find acceptance in the United States. And some of the most successful black artists of the twentieth century worked and studied in France in order to further their art careers.

Sculptor Meta Vaux Warrick Fuller was one such artist. She moved to Paris in 1899 to study sculpture at the Académie Colarossi and drawing at the École des Beaux-Arts (School of Fine Arts). Although she was only twenty-two at the time, Fuller's work was admired by famed French artist Auguste Rodin whose statue *The Thinker* is one of the most famous sculptures in the world. With Rodin's encouragement, Fuller entered the prestigious Paris art exhibition known as the Salon in 1903. The Salon, attended by some of the most influential artists and art buyers in the world, is known for its famously tough judges but Fuller's masterpiece *The Wretched* was accepted for the show.

The French judges doubtlessly appreciated the emotional impact of *The Wretched*. Each of the seven figures in the sculpture represents a form of human misery. They include a deformed child, an old man sickened by hunger, a woman who lost her loved ones, and a woman driven insane by sorrow.

After moving back to the United States in 1909, Fuller married a Liberian physician, and moved to Framingham, Massachusetts. Against the strong disapproval of her husband, Fuller

Ethiopia Awakening, by Meta Vaux Warrick Fuller, symbolizes the emergence of the New Negro from her African roots.

single-handedly built her own sculpture studio. Within its walls, she explored what historian Benjamin Brawley calls "the tragedy of the Negro race."[71]

Fuller's artwork was inspired by the Pan-African philosophy of W.E.B. Du Bois, whom she met in Paris in 1900. Pan-Africanism connected black Americans with their African legacy and led Fuller to create the sculpture *Ethiopia Awakening* in 1913. This bronze sculpture symbolizes the emergence of the New Negro from her African roots. Her legs and lower torso are wrapped like a mummy but a beautiful black woman with long flowing hair and the headdress of an Egyptian queen emerges from the binding. The symbolism of the sculpture is explored by curator David Driskell and his coauthors in their book *Harlem Renaissance: Art of Black America*. They write,

> *Ethiopia Awakening* was a truly Pan-Africanist work of art. At a time when Picasso ... gleaned design elements from the art of non-Western societies without being responsible for the cultural context out of which the work came, Fuller's art [demonstrated the] ... union between Black Africa and Black America.... The symbol of Africa who reaches forth from bondage to freedom connotes the awakening of the forces of good, truth, and beauty in rebellion against ... [the white] exploitation of African peoples and resources.[72]

As a black female artist working during an era of excessive racism and sexism, Fuller keenly understood the concept of breaking free from restraints. This theme was once again displayed in the 1919 sculpture *Mary Turner* (*Silent Protest Against Mob Violence*). But unlike *Ethiopia Awakening*, the vision of Mary Turner was based on horrific events.

In 1918 the pregnant Mary Turner was accused of plotting to kill a white man, aided by her husband and two other black men in Valdosta, Georgia. Although the accusations were false, Turner and the three men were lynched, burned, and their bodies were riddled with bullets. In the aftermath, thousands of African Americans marched in a silent protest down Fifth Avenue in New York. Fuller was deeply moved by the demonstration and "memorialized the awakening defiance of her people in her sculpture.... *Mary Turner* ... a poignant portrayal of a woman struggling to define and free herself,"[73] according to Mary Schmidt Campbell, executive director of the Studio Museum in Harlem.

Although Fuller never lived in Harlem, her work inspired Manhattan-based artist Augusta Savage, another female sculptor who struggled against chauvinism and bigotry. Beyond the art world, many writers, musicians, and dancers of the 1920s admired Fuller's spirit and style which symbolized the emergence of the New Negro. As Campbell writes, Fuller was "one of the most important precursors to the Renaissance."[74] And she continued to create profoundly beautiful works until her death in 1968.

Augusta Savage

Sculptor Augusta Savage was a renowned artist and educator as the following excerpt from the North by South Web site explains:

Augusta Savage was born on February 29, 1892 in Green Cove Springs, Florida. Augusta knew at an early age that she wanted to become a sculptor. Unfortunately, Savage's father, a Methodist minister, disapproved of his daughter's love for art because he believed her creations were pagan. As a result, Augusta experienced periods in her life when she was unable to practice her sculpting.... In 1921, Augusta Savage moved to New York believing that the North would provide her with the artistic opportunity she desired....

When Augusta Savage reached Harlem, it did not take long for her to establish herself not only as an artist, but also as a teacher. Most of Savage's sculptures, in some way, reflect an aspect of African-American culture. For example, *The Harp* was a sculpture influenced by Negro spirituals and hymns, most notably James Weldon Johnson's "Lift Every Voice and Sing." Ms. Savage was unique from other artists in that most of her sculptures focused on black [facial features]. This is readily seen in a sculpture of her nephew entitled *Gamin*....

In 1932, Augusta established the Savage Studio of Arts and Crafts at 163 West 143rd Street. Savage used this studio as a way to provide adults with art education. In 1937, she became the first director of the Harlem Community Arts Center, an institution funded by the Works Progress Administration (WPA). The Arts Center was a place where African Americans could learn about their culture through the study of fine arts.

"Augusta Savage," *North by South*, http://northbysouth.kenyon.edu/1998/art/pages/savage.htm.

Something New and Modern

Like Fuller, painter Aaron Douglas worked with a European master and was strongly influenced by the design elements of African art and African American imagery. Douglas embarked on a successful painting career after moving from Topeka, Kansas, to Harlem in 1925 at the age of twenty-six. In New York, his drawings greatly impressed German painter and designer Winold Reiss, who gave Douglas a full scholarship to his art school. Reiss encouraged Douglas to turn away from the European art traditions he learned in school and urged him to "express racial commitment to his art."[75] Douglas did so,

The Negro in an African Setting *is one panel from Aaron Douglas's 1933 four-panel work* Aspects of Negro Life.

exploring issues of race, slavery, and the role of black Americans in the modern world.

Douglas's work cleverly combines several art styles that were extremely popular. He drew on the influences of art deco, a style characterized by geometric forms, sweeping curves, and models with elongated torsos. Douglas was also inspired by Picasso's cubism and the art nouveau genre, which utilized organic forms found in nature such as vines,

Aspects of Negro Life

When Aaron Douglas painted the four-panel series *Aspects of Negro Life* at the New York Public Library in Harlem, he wanted to depict a Pan-African message and connect African American culture to Africa while educating the viewer about black history.

The first panel, *The Negro in an African Setting*, depicts the action of a silhouetted couple dancing in a tribal circle. This is meant to emphasize the importance of dance and music in black culture. This joyous scene is followed by *Into Bondage*, depicting proud Africans in chains glumly walking to slave ships as a beam of light shines down on one figure who looks to the sky and seems to be asking "Why?"

The most intricate panel, *From Slavery to Reconstruction*, shows slaves picking cotton on the left side of the painting, while a trumpet player and dancer perform on the right. The slaves are tormented by Klansmen on horses painted in hellish tones of red, orange, and brown. A black politician is making a speech in the center of the painting, while Civil War soldiers march in the background. As is typical in Douglas's work, buildings, such as a factory and the U.S. Capitol, are painted as majestic but unattainable.

The final panel from *Aspects of Negro Life, Song of the Towers*, presents a saxophone player as an icon of jazz music. This figure represents the melding of African heritage, African American culture, and black national identity. Like the other panels of the series, it is painted with Douglas's trademark shadings of concentric circles and angular beams of light.

leaves, flowers, birds, and the human form. Describing his style, Douglas stated:

I wanted to create something new and modern that fitted in with Art Deco and the other things that were taking the country by storm. That is how I came upon the notion to use a number of things such as Cubism and a style with straight lines to emphasize the mathematical relationship of things.[76]

Many of Douglas's angular, stylized figures are presented as silhouettes. The figures are painted with bodies forward but faces in profile—heads turned to the side. However, the single eye is drawn as if viewed from the front, not the side. This style is seen in ancient Egyptian art and referred to as the Egyptian form by Douglas.

The Vision of African Americans

Shortly after his arrival in Harlem, Douglas met Du Bois, who hired him to work in the mailroom at *Crisis*. Within weeks, however, Douglas was drawing illustrations for articles in the NAACP newspaper. After seeing the quality of his work, Alain Locke commissioned Douglas to create illustrations for *The New Negro*, a book that played a central role in the Harlem Renaissance. Soon after, Charles S. Johnson, who had originally encouraged Douglas to move to New York, began using the artist's work in *Opportunity*.

With the three founding fathers of the renaissance acting as mentors and patrons, Douglas quickly recognized that he was about to become a major success. Barely keeping his ego in check, he began to vocalize the Pan-African views of black cultural superiority. In a letter to his future wife, Alta Sawyer, in late 1925 he said,

> At my present rate of progress I'll be a giant in two years, I want to be frightful to look at. A veritable black terror. They (White America) believe that a black artist is impossible. They have good grounds for their belief. Most of us are utterly despicable. Most of us feel that we have reached the heights when we have depicted their chalky faces and disgusting sentimentality or filled yards of canvas with feeble imitations of their second rate "little masters."[77]

Douglas's attitudes undoubtedly endeared him to Harlem's literati. Before long he moved into Niggerati Manor with Zora Neale Hurston, Wallace Thurman, and other Harlem bohemians. He also became friends with Langston Hughes and began illustrating his poems on the pages of *Fire!!* After moving out of the manor, Douglas rented his own apartment which became the center of social activity for the writers, artists, dancers, musicians, poets, and playwrights of the New Negro movement.

Despite his lively social life, Douglas worked tirelessly to create indelible images during the Harlem Renaissance. In addition to his newspaper and magazine work, he illustrated book covers for James Weldon Johnson's *The Autobiography of an Ex-Colored Man*, Thurman's *The Blacker the Berry*, and Claude McKay's *Home to Harlem*. These designs feature Douglas's unique flat, silhouetted figures, the lines drawn in such a way as to give a sense of movement to the characters.

The sharp contrasting colors of Douglas's book cover illustrations were softened considerably in a series of paintings that he created at the request of Weldon Johnson for his book of poems *God's Trombones: Seven Negro Sermons in Verse*. The book was inspired by Bible stories, black spirituals, recent African American history, and black American culture. The paintings, including *Noah's Ark, Study for God's Trombones,* and *The Crucifixion,* are executed in monochromatic tones. For example,

God's Trombones, which depicts a silhouette of a black man standing among jungle foliage and struggling with chains, is created in tones of light and dark blue. *The Crucifixion*, with a black man struggling under the weight of a giant cross, is done in various tones of purple. Painted in the style of cubism and the forms of African sculpture, these canvases showed Douglas as a pioneering artist who invented his own painting genre. Curator Susan Earle writes,

> In these complex compositions that tell deep stories, Douglas layers transparent, geometric rays and graduated circles of light over streamlined forms, such as the great boat hull and animals in *Noah's Ark*. The potent head in profile with a cut-in eye imparts a mysterious focus to the image … [suggesting] that the vision of African Americans portrayed is a commanding force for change, and for a new embracing energy that could unite the world.[78]

True Jazz Age Atmosphere

The paintings for *God's Trombones* sparked an increased demand for Douglas's work. While he continued to illustrate for publications, 1927 marked the artist's first large-scale public work, a mural for the new nightspot Club Ebony in Harlem. Unveiled upon the Club's opening on October 5, the mural, long since destroyed, was filled with Pan-African cultural symbols in contrast with nature and the modern world. These characteristic elements of a Douglas painting were described in a 1927 article in the newspaper *Kansas City Call* quoted in *Aaron Douglas*: "There are tropical settings of huge trees and flowers, figures of African tom-tom players and dancers, pictures of the American Negro with a banjo and in cakewalk [dance]. On the main panel silhouetted against a background of modern skyscrapers are the forms of contemporary race dancers and musicians."[79]

The mural was a visual history of black music. And some of the so-called race dancers and musicians painted beneath the skyscrapers were in attendance on opening night. Florence Mills, just back from a whirlwind European tour, was the guest of honor. Other luminaries included Mac Rae and his Ten Ebony Stompers, Ethel Waters, Paul Robeson, W.E.B. Du Bois, and Wallace Thurman. According to one reporter, Douglas's painting decorated Club Ebony in "true Jazz Age atmosphere [and the] elite of Harlem … kept the swank new club packed until five in the morning. Gorgeous gowns, furs, shawls, and jewels vied with the elegance of thick velvet carpets and sunken damask upholstery while surrounding all were the startling blues, reds, yellows, and blacks of Aaron Douglas's painted jungle and jazzboes [jazz musicians]."[80]

The 1929 stock market crash soon put an end to such glittering Harlem scenes. But by 1930 Douglas was so

Artist Aaron Douglas's distinctive style made him one of the most popular artists of the Harlem Renaissance.

well established that he called the first year of the Depression his most successful year ever. While many of Harlem's performers, artists, and authors struggled to make ends meet, Douglas thrived, producing seven murals in seven years between 1930 and 1937. Critics consider these public paintings to be among the artist's best. And some of them might never have been painted if not for the Depression.

Throughout the 1930s, President Roosevelt's New Deal programs provided WPA art grants to public institutions such as libraries and historically black colleges and universities. One such grant in 1933 paid for Douglas to create a four-panel series called *Aspects of Negro Life* at the New York Public Library in Harlem (now the Schomburg Center for Research in Black Culture). The four paintings follow the

Photographing the Renaissance

Many of the enduring images of the Harlem Renaissance were captured on film by James VanDerZee. Like the painters and sculptors of the time, VanDerZee, was motivated by the New Negro philosophy. His photos depict African Americans in poses that show self-respect, style, and optimism.

"Couple Wearing Raccoon Coats" is one of VanDerZee's most famous pictures, and one that encapsulates the era. The picture of a man and a woman posed with their expensive automobile presents a picture of black upper-class life rarely seen in the United States at that time. This was among many of VanDerZee's photographs showing African Americans in pursuit of the American Dream at sporting events, family gatherings, funerals, weddings, and barbershops. VanDerZee photographed black celebrities such as Marcus Garvey, heavyweight champion Jack Johnson, dancer Bill "Bojangles" Robinson, and singers Florence Mills and Mamie Smith. Working out of his studio, Guarantee Photo, on 135th Street, VanDerZee also shot portraits of families, babies, brides, and grooms. His signature technique involved using darkroom tricks and double exposures to give his portraits an interesting edge. For example, "Wedding Portrait with the Superimposed Image of a Little Girl," shows a shadowy youngster holding a doll at the feet of the bride and groom, symbolizing the predicted future of the couple.

VanDerZee was also a dedicated musician, playing the piano with such jazz giants as Fletcher Henderson. But he will always be remembered for his indelible photographs that preserve the dignity, independence, and joy of the Harlem residents during the renaissance.

history of African Americans from their free lives in Africa to their enslavement in the United States. They also depict scenes from the Reformation period after the Civil War, the Great Migration to northern cities, and the Depression.

Douglas also painted murals at Fisk University in Nashville, Tennessee, where he took a job as assistant professor of art education in 1938. He taught painting at Fisk until his retirement in 1966 and died in Nashville in 1979. Although he spent the last half of his life in Tennessee, Douglas will always be remembered as the "pioneering Africanist [and] the father of Black American art,"[81] a title bequeathed on him by Locke.

Folk Expression and Satire

While Aaron Douglas dominated the art scene during the Harlem Renaissance, there were others whose work was based on black American life, culture, legend, and tradition. Many of these artists were introduced to the public through exhibits sponsored by the Harmon Foundation. This prestigious organization, named for white art patron William E. Harmon, began awarding prizes for achievement in art in 1926.

Harmon Foundation exhibitions were seen all over New York City, and these shows provided African American artists with widespread exposure to the general public. The publicity attracted black artists from across the country, and the number of artists in the foundation registry grew from about 10 in 1926 to over 300 in 1929.

Palmer Hayden worked as a custodian at the Harmon Foundation to pay for art supplies. He won a Harmon Foundation Gold Award for Distinguished Achievement in Fine Arts in 1926 with the painting *Fetiche et Fleures* (*Fetish and Flowers*). This work is a still life of an African mask, or fetish from Gabon; a tablecloth from the Congo; and a table with a vase of flowers. Like other painters at the time, Hayden used symbols of Africa to explore the roots of black American art.

Hayden's contributions to the Harlem Renaissance included depictions of African subjects in their humble homes, scenes from black folk stories, life in the rural South, and life in Harlem. Hayden had grown up in Wide Water, Virginia, and his childhood memories of small-town residents informed many of his paintings.

Hayden generated great controversy with his images that portrayed African Americans with cartoonish, exaggerated features and grins reminiscent of blackface minstrel shows. His subjects, such as those in *Nous Quatre à Paris* (*Us Four in Paris*), often had round, bald heads and large eyes, noses, ears, and lips. Art historian James A. Porter considered these paintings tasteless and said Hayden's work pandered to racist appetites for stereotypical images of black people. However, Locke defended Hayden, believing he was part of a group of young artists who were inspired by the New Negro movement "and its

The Janitor Who Paints *by Palmer Hayden. Hayden's art included scenes of Africans in their homes.*

crusade of folk expression in all the arts."[82] Hayden himself explained that black people sometimes acted like minstrel clowns, wearing expressions like those in his paintings to hide their true feelings when in the presence of white people.

In 1932 Hayden was signed to a WPA program for the U.S. Treasury Art Project. His assignment, which paid thirty dollars a week, was to paint scenes of daily life in Harlem. One of the most enduring images from this series is the 1938 *Midsummer Night in Harlem*, which shows dozens of figures sitting on stoops in front of Harlem row houses, leaning out apartment windows, or driving in cars. The dark faces and bright white teeth of the characters offended Porter who said the painting reminded him of old-time posters for minstrel shows that used to be plastered on buildings and fences in the city. However, Hayden considered the work satire, saying the humorous and ironic depictions were meant to mock white stereotypes.

Hayden's most renowned work consists of a series of paintings about the folk hero John Henry created between 1944 and 1954. Henry was a steel-driving man, whose ability to lay track for railroads was legendary. Henry entered into a competition with a steam-powered drill, trying to drive in more spikes and beat the machine. John Henry died with his hammer in his hand after winning the contest.

Hayden immortalized John Henry's story on twelve canvases. Commenting on the series, he said, Henry was "a powerful and popular working man who belonged to my section of the country and to my own race."[83] The critically acclaimed series helped Hayden achieve widespread respect, and in later years his work was displayed at prestigious galleries such as the Whitney in New York and the Smithsonian in Washington, D.C. While many people missed the satire in Hayden's early images, they were based on the double-consciousness philosophy of Du Bois, who wrote that blacks were continually forced to look at themselves through the eyes of their oppressors.

"Primitiveness and Tradition"

Like Hayden, artist William C. Johnson often attracted controversy. Although he was trained as a traditional academic painter at the National Academy of Design in New York, he painted in what is known as the primitive, folk, or naive style. Artists who work in this genre deliberately create crude images that resemble the drawings of children. When a critic asked Johnson why he abandoned his training as a talented academic painter, he replied, "My aim is to express in a natural way what I feel both rhythmically and spiritually, all that has been saved up in my family of primitiveness and tradition."[84]

Johnson's primitivism did not come directly from African American traditions. Ironically, it is heavily influenced by the time he spent in Europe studying the expressionist movement that developed in Germany. Norwegian painter Edvard Munch is one of the founders of expressionism. His 1893 painting, *The Scream*, is a classic of the genre, depicting a simply drawn character standing on a bridge with his mouth wide open and his hands covering his ears.

William H. Johnson's art made use of bold colors with an almost cartoon-like quality, as shown here in his work Chain Gang.

Johnson used expressionism combined with an almost cartoonlike technique in brightly colored paintings such as *Chain Gang, Young Man in a Vest, Café,* and *Li'l Sis.* These paintings are commentaries not only on the positive aspects of

African American life, but also on the social troubles faced by black Americans.

Like many other artists of the Harlem Renaissance, Johnson received less attention and adulation than the authors, singers, musicians, and dancers. However, artwork by Johnson, Douglas, Hayden, Augusta Savage, Richmond Barthe, Archibald Motley, and Loïs Mailou Jones provide a priceless visual record of the Jazz Age and the Harlem Renaissance.

Epilogue

An End and a Beginning

The Harlem Renaissance is remembered as a time of great creativity, when black writers, musicians, and artists helped change widespread attitudes about African Americans. As Langston Hughes described it, "some Harlemites . . . thought the race problem had at last been solved through Art… . They were sure the New Negro would lead a new life from then on in green pastures of tolerance."[85] And it was true that black authors during the renaissance were published more often, and Broadway plays with all-black casts were largely successful. However, there was a naivety in the belief that things would change for the better and Hughes himself pointed out that the "ordinary Negro hadn't heard of the Negro Renaissance. And if they had it hadn't raised their wages any."[86] And with the onset of the Great Depression at the end of 1929, those already low wages fell dramatically, more than 43 percent in four years.

In 1933 another economic disaster hit when Prohibition was repealed. The white patrons who flocked to Harlem speakeasies to buy bootleg liquor could now obtain legal drinks in their own neighborhoods. While some Harlem speakeasies converted to legitimate bars, many shut their doors, laying off untold numbers of black waiters, waitresses, busboys, cooks, bartenders, dancers, musicians, managers, and more.

By 1935 nearly half of all Harlem residents were unemployed. The high rents in Harlem had not gone down, however, and many single apartments were now occupied by two or three families. Harlem quickly turned from "The World's Greatest Negro Metropolis" into an inner city slum. The hard times created an exodus among the elite of the Harlem Renaissance. Black writers and literary promoters such as Hughes, James Weldon Johnson, Charles S. Johnson, and W.E.B. Du Bois fled New York City, many relocating to Paris.

The bleak economic conditions in Harlem did not stop the migration of poor, uneducated African Americans from the South. Between 1930 and 1935 another seventy-seven thousand black migrants entered New York, most of them settling in Harlem. The poverty, hopelessness, and overcrowding created great stress and was blamed for the full-blown riot that exploded in Harlem on March 19, 1935. It began when police arrested a Puerto Rican boy for stealing a ten-cent pocketknife from a white-owned business. Rumors spread that the boy was beaten to death by police and looting began. By the next day, two hundred stores had been burned to the ground, three African Americans were dead, hundreds were injured, and nearly 2 million dollars worth of property was destroyed. In reality, the Puerto Rican boy had been released by police before the riot began when the shopkeeper decided not to press charges.

Black Power

Even with its violence and economic hardships, Harlem was largely invisible to most Americans throughout the Depression and World War II. But the influence of the Harlem Renaissance remained strong. In the decades that followed, literature from the era inspired best-selling black authors like Ralph Ellison and Richard Wright to explore African American life. It also served to inspire modern writers such as Toni Morrison and Alice Walker. The outstanding jazz music of Duke Ellington, Eubie Blake, and others set a standard by which all other jazz music was measured in later years. And the political aspects of the Harlem Renaissance influenced a new generation of black leaders in the 1950s and 1960s. Nation of Islam leader Malcolm X and civil rights icon Martin Luther King Jr. both credited Marcus Garvey and founders of the New Negro movement for redefining black consciousness. And the progress of the era served as a starting point from which African Americans gained a spirit of self-determination and pride. In the mid-1960s this was expressed as Black Power and through the expression "Black is Beautiful." Although it lasted little more than a decade, the Harlem Renaissance highlighted the important contributions that African Americans—and millions of black people throughout the world—have made to American art, society, and culture. And the world today would be a drab and different place if that rebirth of the black arts had never happened.

Notes

Introduction: A Rebirth of Black Culture

1. Paul Laurence Dunbar, *The Sport of the Gods*. Charleston, SC: BiblioBazaar, 2007, p. 47.
2. Cary D. Wintz, *Black Culture and the Harlem Renaissance*. Houston, TX: Rice University Press, 1988, p. 3.

Chapter One: The New Negro Movement

3. Leon Litwack, *Trouble in Mind: Black Southerners in the Age of Jim Crow*. New York: Knopf, 1998, p. xiv.
4. Quoted in Jervis Anderson, *This Was Harlem*. New York: Farrar Straus Giroux, 1982, p. 53.
5. Quoted in Anderson, *This Was Harlem*, p. 56.
6. James Weldon Johnson, "The Making of Harlem," *Survey Graphic*, March 1925, http://etext.virginia.edu/harlem/JohMakiF.html.
7. James Weldon Johnson, "The Making of Harlem," March 1925, Alain Locke, ed., *The New Negro: An Interpretation*. New York: Atheneum, 1969, p. 308.
8. Quoted in Tim Brooks and Richard Keith Spottswood, *Lost Sounds: Blacks and the Birth of the Recording Industry, 1890–1919*. Chicago: University of Illinois Press, 2004, p. 280.
9. Quoted in Theodore G. Vincent, ed., *Voices of a Black Nation*. Trenton, NJ: Africa World, 1973, p. 68.

10. Quoted in Vincent, *Voices of a Black Nation*, p. 65.
11. Quoted in Vincent, *Voices of a Black Nation*, p. 69.
12. Quoted in Elton C. Fax, *Garvey: The Story of a Pioneer Black Nationalist*. New York: Dodd, Mead, 1972, p. 103.
13. Marcus Garvey and Herbert Aptheker et al., eds., *The Marcus Garvey and Universal Negro Improvement Association Papers*, vol. 2. Berkeley: University of California Press, 1983, pp. 297–298.
14. Quoted in Garvey and Aptheker et al., *The Marcus Garvey and Universal Negro Improvement Association Papers*, p. 493.
15. William Edward Burghardt Du Bois and David L. Lewis, *W.E.B. Du Bois: A Reader*, New York: Macmillan, 1995, p. 333.
16. Quoted in Vincent, *Voices of a Black Nation*, p. 96.
17. Quoted in Theodore Kornweibel Jr., *Seeing Red: Federal Campaigns Against Black Militancy, 1919–1925*. Bloomington: Indiana University Press, 1998, p. 102.

Chapter Two: The Literary Crowd

18. W.E.B. Du Bois, *The Souls of Black Folk*. Chicago: McClurg, 1903, www.bartleby.com/114/1.html .

19. Langston Hughes, *The Fight for Freedom: The Story of the NAACP*. New York: Norton, 1962, p. 203.

20. James Weldon Johnson, *Along This Way: The Autobiography of James Weldon Johnson*. New York: Viking, 1933, p. 203.

21. Quoted in Wayne F. Cooper, *Claude McKay: Rebel Sojourner in the Harlem Renaissance*. Baton Rouge: Louisiana State University Press, 1987, p. 68.

22. Claude McKay, *Harlem Shadows: The Poems of Claude McKay*. New York: Harcourt Brace, 1922.

23. Quoted in Cooper, *Claude McKay*, p. 164.

24. James Weldon Johnson, ed., *The Book of American Negro Poetry*. New York: Harcourt Brace, 1922, www.bartleby.com/269/1000.html.

25. Quoted in Cary D. Wintz, ed., *Harlem Speaks: A Living History of the Harlem Renaissance*. Naperville, IL: Sourcebooks, 2007, p. 354.

26. Langston Hughes, "The Weary Blues," Knopf, 1926, http://cai.ucdavis.edu/uccp/workingweary.html.

27. Langston Hughes, *The Big Sea*. New York: Hill and Wang, 1993, pp. 266–267.

28. Quoted in Hughes, *The Big Sea*, p. 266.

29. Hughes, *The Big Sea*, p. 267.

30. Quoted in Arna Bontemps, ed., *The Harlem Renaissance Remembered*. New York: Dodd, Mead, 1972, pp. 64–65.

31. Quoted in Bontemps, *The Harlem Renaissance Remembered*, p. 67.

32. Quoted in David Levering Lewis, *When Harlem Was in Vogue*. New York: Knopf, 1981, p. 124.

33. Quoted in Lewis, *When Harlem Was in Vogue*, p. 125.

34. Alain Locke, ed., *The New Negro*. New York: Atheneum, 1969, p. xvii.

35. Quoted in Steven Watson, *The Harlem Renaissance*. New York: Pantheon, 1995, p. 89.

36. Hughes, *The Big Sea*, p. 235.

37. Quoted in Wintz, *Black Culture and the Harlem Renaissance*, p. 83.

38. Quoted in Hughes, *The Big Sea*, p. 235.

Chapter Three: The Jazz Age

39. Quoted in Samuel A. Floyd Jr., ed., *Black Music in the Harlem Renaissance*. New York: Greenwood, 1990, p. 2.

40. Hughes, *The Big Sea*, pp. 224–225.

41. Hughes, *The Big Sea*, p. 225.

42. Mark C. Gridley, *Jazz Styles: History and Analysis*. Englewood Cliffs, NJ: Prentice Hall, 1988, p. 66.

43. Quoted in Alyn Shipton, *A New History of Jazz*. New York: Continuum, 2001, p. 267.

44. Mark Tucker, "The Renaissance Education of Duke Ellington," Floyd, *Black Music in the Harlem Renaissance*, p. 111.

45. Wintz, *Harlem Speaks*, p. 36.

46. Hughes, *The Big Sea*, p. 226.

47. Langston Hughes and Milton Meltzer, *Black Magic*. Englewood Cliffs, NJ: Prentice Hall, 1967, p. 80.

48. Quoted in Wintz, *Harlem Speaks*, pp. 179–180.

49. Anderson, *This Was Harlem*, p. 309.

Chapter Four: The Renaissance in Black Theater

50. Hughes, *The Big Sea*, p. 223.

51. Hughes, *The Big Sea*, p. 223.

52. David Krasner, *A Beautiful Pageant*. New York: Palgrave Macmillan, 2003, p. 229.

53. Hughes and Meltzer, *Black Magic*, p. 123.

54. Quoted in Krasner, *A Beautiful Pageant*, p. 230.

55. James Weldon Johnson, *Black Manhattan*. New York: Da Capo, 1991, p. 170.
56. Quoted in Krasner, *A Beautiful Pageant*, p. 189.
57. Allen Woll, *Black Musical Theatre: From Coontown to Dreamgirls*. Baton Rouge: Louisiana State University, 1989, p. 60.
58. Quoted in Krasner, *A Beautiful Pageant*, p. 241.
59. Quoted in Al Rose, *Eubie Blake*. New York: Schirmer, 1979, p. 74.
60. Quoted in Woll, *Black Musical Theatre*, p. 65.
61. Quoted in Lewis, *When Harlem Was in Vogue*, p. 96.
62. Roy Parker Jr., "Paul Green's Legacy," Paul Green Foundation, May 2003, www.ibiblio.org/paulgreen/paulgreenlegacy.html.
63. Hughes and Meltzer, *Black Magic*, p. 113.
64. Lewis, *When Harlem Was in Vogue*, p. 207.
65. Lewis, *When Harlem Was in Vogue*, p. 207.
66. Lewis, *When Harlem Was in Vogue*, p. 207.
67. "New Plays in Manhattan," *Time*, February 20, 1928, www.time.com/time/magazine/article/0,9171,731637,00.html.
68. Quoted in Johnson, *Black Manhattan*, p. 219.
69. Quoted in Rose, *Eubie Blake*, pp. 109–110.

Chapter Five: A Renaissance in Art

70. Quoted in Cary D. Wintz, ed., *The Harlem Renaissance 1920–1940*, vol. 2, *The Politics and Aesthetics of "New Negro" Literature*. New York: Garland, 1996, p. 198.
71. Benjamin Brawley, *Women of Achievement*. Chicago, IL: Woman's American Baptist Home Mission Society, 1919, p. 68.
72. Mary Schmidt Campbell, David Driskell et al., *Harlem Renaissance: Art of Black America*. New York: Abrams, 1987, pp. 108–109.
73. Campbell et al., *Harlem Renaissance*, p. 27.
74. Campbell et al., *Harlem Renaissance*, p. 25.
75. Quoted in Campbell et al., *Harlem Renaissance*, p. 110.
76. Quoted in Susan Earle, ed., *Aaron Douglas: African American Modernist*. Lawrence, KS: Spencer Museum of Art, 2007, pp. 89–90.
77. Quoted in Earle, *Aaron Douglas*, p. 83.
78. Earle, *Aaron Douglas*, p. 23.
79. Quoted in Earle, *Aaron Douglas*, p. 212.
80. Quoted in Bill Egan, *Florence Mills: Harlem Jazz Queen*. Lanham, MD: Scarecrow, 2004, p. 218.
81. Quoted in Campbell et al., *Harlem Renaissance*, p. 110.
82. Quoted in Eric Hanks, "Journey from the Crossroads: Palmer Hayden's Right Turn," *International Review of African American Art* 16, no. 1, pp. 30–42, www.mhanksgallery.com/hayart.html.
83. Quoted in Theresa A. Leininger-Miller, *New Negro Artists in Paris*. New Brunswick, NJ: Rutgers University Press, 2000, p. 97.
84. Quoted in Campbell et al., *Harlem Renaissance*, p. 135.

Epilogue: An End and a Beginning

85. Hughes, *The Big Sea*, p. 228.
86. Hughes, *The Big Sea*, p. 228.

For More Information

Books

Wendy Hart Beckman, *Artists and Writers of the Harlem Renaissance*. Berkeley Heights, NJ: Enslow, 2002. This book presents biographies of key Harlem Renaissance innovators, including James Weldon Johnson, Alain LeRoy Locke, Zora Neale Hurston, Bessie Smith, Aaron Douglas, Duke Ellington, Langston Hughes, Countee Cullen, and Josephine Baker.

Carin T. Ford, *Duke Ellington: "I Live with Music."* Berkeley Heights, NJ: Enslow, 2008. This is the story of Edward "Duke" Ellington and how he became famous for composing, conducting, and playing jazz music inspired by African American culture.

Jennifer Blizin Gillis, *W.E.B. Dubois*. Chicago: Heinemann, 2006. This book explores the life and accomplishments of W.E.B. Du Bois, one of the founding fathers of the Pan-African movement and leader of the NAACP.

Brenda Haugen, *Langston Hughes: The Voice of Harlem*. Minneapolis, MN: Compass Point, 2006. This is a biography of Langston Hughes, one of the leading literary geniuses of the Harlem Renaissance.

Laban Carrick Hill, *Harlem Stomp!* New York: Megan Tingley, 2003. This cultural history of the Harlem Renaissance is told in the colorful, energetic, and exciting tone of the times.

Langston Hughes, *The Big Sea*. New York: Hill and Wang, 1993. Langston Hughes, the leading author of the Harlem Renaissance, presents his life story as a series of episodes that read like short stories, written in his unique rhythmic "jazz" style.

Laura Baskes Litwin, *Zora Neale Hurston: "I've Been in Sorrow's Kitchen."* Berkeley Heights, NJ: Enslow, 2008. This is a profile of the influential writer Zora Neale Hurston with a focus on her anthropological studies of African American culture in the South, the folklore she collected, and her use of it in her stories.

Web Sites

Circle Association (www.math.buffalo.edu/~sww/circle/harlem-ren-sites.html). A site with extensive information about the Harlem Renaissance with biographies, a timeline, book excerpts, and links to many other sites.

Drop Me Off in Harlem (http://artsedge.kennedy-center.org/exploring/harlem/artsedge.html). A project of the John F. Kennedy Center for the Performing Arts, this site has photos, biographies, and other interesting features concerning the actors, musicians, artists, dancers, and writers of the Harlem Renaissance.

North by South (http://northbysouth. kenyon.edu/1998/index.htm). This Web site is based on a yearlong seminar by the National Endowment for the Humanities that researched the migration of African Americans from the South to the North. It includes information about Harlem's jazz, art, medical practices, and education and how they were influenced by black Southern culture.

SallyGaster's Phat African American Library (www.math.buffalo.edu/~sww/ Snally_Gaster.html). This site contains links to the works of the Harlem Renaissance poets, including Arna Bontemps, Langston Hughes, Georgia Douglas Johnson, Jean Toomer, Countee Cullen, and Claude McKay.

Harlem: Mecca of the New Negro (http://etext.virginia.edu/harlem). In March 1925, the popular magazine *Survey Graphic* dedicated a special issue to the Harlem Renaissance. This Web site contains all the original articles from the issue by Alain Locke, James Weldon Johnson, W.E.B. Du Bois, Countee Cullen, and others of renown. The original pages of the issue, with photographs, are also available on this site.

VG: Voices from the Gaps (http://voices. cla.umn.edu/vg/Bios/entries/ hurston_zora_neale.html). This Web site offers a good biography of Zora Neale Hurston with related links, photographs, and a selected biography of her books.

Index

Picture Credits

Text Credits

"The Weary Blues," excerpted from Langston Hughes, *The Collected Poems of Langston Hughes*, New York, NY: Knopf, 1994. Edited by Arnold Rampersad with David Roessel, Associate Editor. Copyright © 1994 by The Estate of Langston Hughes. Used by permission of Alfred A. Knopf, a division of Random House, Inc. Reprinted in the British Commonwealth by permission of Harold Ober Associates Incorporated.

About the Author

Stuart A. Kallen is the prolific author of more than 250 nonfiction books for children and young adults. He has written on topics ranging from the theory of relativity to the history of world music. In addition, Kallen has written award-winning children's videos and television scripts. In his spare time, he is a singer/songwriter/guitarist in San Diego, California.